Last of a BReed

To Hoppie,

Keep cheering for the Cards!

Love from Ann and me!

Billy Reed

03-24-2019

Last of a BReed

A Legendary Kentucky Writer's Journey
Through Six Decades of Sports and Journalism

Billy Reed

Acclaim Press
MORLEY, MISSOURI

Acclaim Press
— Your Next Great Book —

P.O. Box 238
Morley, MO 63767
(573) 472-9800
www.acclaimpress.com

Book Design: Rodney Atchley
Cover Design: M. Frene Melton

ISBN: 978-1-948901-00-0 / 1-948901-00-5
Library of Congress Control Number: 2018904459

First Printing 2018
Printed in the United States of America
10 9 8 7 6 5 4 3 2 1

This publication was produced using available information.
The publisher regrets it cannot assume responsibility for errors or omissions.

CONTENTS

FOREWORD

So many times I've called Billy Reed for so many things. It was April, 1981, when I asked for Bob Knight's phone number.

"What's up?" Billy said.

"There's a rumor he might retire and do color for CBS," I said.

My bosses at the Washington Post had asked me to check out the story. I had Knight's office number, but it was 1 a.m.

If being awakened by the phone at 1 in the morning is seldom fun, I am here to say it is never fun to make a phone call at 1 in the morning to a basketball coach famous for roaring belligerence.

Me: "Bob, the AP is running a story that says…."

Knight: "And you're calling NOW to ask about that?"

Me: "I can't write a rumor. I'm doing what you say reporters never do. Making a phone call."

Knight: "There's no story, I've got nothing to say."

Me: "OK."

Knight, suddenly: "HOW'D YOU GET MY NUMBER?"

Me: "Billy said you wouldn't mind."

Knight, roaring: "DAMMIT."

Billy and I met in 1966. We were ambitious kids. I was a small-town Illinoisan, 25 years old, Billy a small-town Kentuckian, 23. It was a thrill to work at the *Louisville Courier-Journal*, then one of America's best newspapers. For the next half-century and more, we were colleagues of the best kind. Not that we always worked for the same organization; we were on the C-J staff together only seven years. What we shared was more meaningful and bound us together for life. We loved reporting and writing. In our minds, journalism came with a capital J.

So, of course, Billy gave me Knight's number.

And why wouldn't he give me that small thing? He'd already given me a big thing. He'd given me Kentucky. This takes some explaining.

Before coming to Louisville in the winter of 1965, I knew almost nothing about Kentucky. I knew a name, Adolph Rupp, and I knew a horse race, the Kentucky Derby.

Before I left Kentucky in 1977, I knew almost everything. I had seen Steve Cauthen, 15 years old, asleep in the hay of a Churchill Downs stall – a babe in a manger. I saw Secretariat fly and Ruffian fall. Two dozen Derby Days, maybe more, always at Billy's side, I walked over from the barns to the paddock with the Majestic Princes and Spectacular Bids. I covered games in Freedom Hall and Kingdom Come High School. Rupp came to know me, sort of; the cantankerous old man once took a call from C-J columnist Dick Fenlon and said, "I know two guys in Louisville, one's Fenlon and one's Kindred. One's a good guy, the other one's a son of a bitch. Which one are you?"

All those memories have their origins in Billy's influence. The book in your hands, a reporter's tour de force, is only the latest proof of Billy's passion for Kentucky. I recognized that devotion early on. To hear Billy talk about his old high school, Lexington's Henry Clay, class of '61, was to hear a boy speak of his first love. I knew that no refugee from Illinois could ever match that. I also knew, if Billy cared that much, there was good reason for me to care.

So every year I criss-crossed the state, driving from Ashland to Paducah to Inez, Monkeys Eyebrow, Egypt, and Mummy. I wrote about Jock Sutherland and Hell for Certain and Bull Hancock. There came a day at a Kentucky-Louisville basketball game when someone, perhaps a passionate reader, shoved a shaving-cream pie in my face. For all that, I owe Billy.

And there was the night Billy made a phone call to my house. It was not 1 a.m. It was 3 a.m.

"Dave, guess where I am," he said.

Behind him I heard raucous noise and the clinking of glasses. He was in Las Vegas.

"I just saw Ann-Margret's show," he said.

This was during a phase in my life when I admitted to, and in columns even boasted of, a fan-boy crush on the actress/singer. As it happened, this phase of my life overlapped a phase in my life known as marriage.

"Who's on the phone?" my wife, Cheryl, said.

"Billy. He's in Vegas. He's seen Ann-Margret."

Cheryl was not amused. As I pulled the blankets tighter against an icy chill that fell across our bedroom, she said, "Tell Billy to lose our phone number."

In the early years at the C-J, Billy and I met in mornings at the sports department in search of stories we could write for the next morning's paper. Nights, done with desk duty, we adjourned across the street to Foch Karem's S&H bar. Days off, we played golf, to use a term loosely, and, to use another term more loosely, we also played basketball.

Ah, basketball. I'd been a point guard in high school. To make up for all those times I had given the ball to our shooters, in my C-J days I never made a pass; every time anyone dared throw me the ball, I shot it. Billy called me "Gatling Gun Dave." I will not describe Billy's game. I will, however, quote him. He wrote the foreword for my book, "Basketball: The Dream Game in Kentucky." There he told about playing for Lexington's Park Methodist Bluejays.

> In one memorable game, I was the only substitute. For three quarters, I sat at one end of the bench, the coach and his small son at the other. Finally, late in the game, with the score tied, the coach beckoned me....
>
> "Reed," said the coach, his face wrinkled in a frown and his eyes fixed on the action on the floor.
>
> "Yeah, coach? Yeah? Yeah?"
>
> "Reed, my son has to go to the bathroom. Take him downstairs, will ya?"

Such a book this is, a kaleidoscopic look at a sportswriter's life and times, moving through colors, shifting shapes across seven decades in what Billy called "a golden era of sportswriting." We hear Bob Knight say, "Billy, I can't be the me that you want to me to be. I have to be the me I want me to be." … We see Billy dancing (!) the Julep Jump (!) with one of Lady Gaga's (!) dancers…Good grief, in learning that Billy and Mitch McConnell were in grade school together, we pause in our otherwise delightful journey to allow ourselves a moment of despair that Mitch didn't become the sportswriter and Billy the politician.

Oh, one more thing, this to be saved in the no-good-deed-goes-unpunished file. Mentioning Knight reminds me of my 1 a.m. phone call in April of 1981. Let's say it had been 1:15 a.m. when Knight roared, "DAMMIT." At 1:30 a.m., my phone rang.

It was Billy, poor Billy, poor blistered-ears Billy.

He said, "I hear you called the coach."

—Dave Kindred, Hall of Fame sports writer
September 1, 2018

Last of a BReed

*A Legendary Kentucky Writer's Journey
Through Six Decades of Sports and Journalism*

Chapter One

BIRTH OF AN INK-STAINED WRETCH

One fine evening when I was in New York City to cover something or other, I fell in with a group of literary giants that included popular sports columnist Mike Lupica of the *New York Daily News*, his news side contemporary Pete Hamill, a couple of network TV personalities, and a couple of ink-stained wretches like myself. To cap a wonderful night of drinking and story-telling, we decided to have a couple of last rounds at Elaine's, which then was the coolest celebrity hangout in the city. Naturally, Elaine met us personally and showed us to a choice table.

When I reached that point where I had to empty the ol' bladder, I called over Elaine — by then I was part of the "in" crowd, you understand — and asked where to find the men's room. To which she replied, with a jerk of her thumb, "Go down to Michael Caine, and take a right." I looked that way, and sure enough, there was the wonderful actor I had seen in so many movies. Before I could get up, Lupica leaned over and said, "There's the title of your book."

I laughed, never dreaming I'd write a book about my adventures in journalism. But here I am, all these years later, trying to leave something of value and interest to my family, friends, and anybody who might be interested in what it was like to work in a golden era of sports writing, using tools and methods that now seem ancient. I'm also writing this book in the hope of encouraging young people who might feel their dreams are impossible due to the circumstances in which they have grown up.

I was born on July 12, 1943, in Mt. Sterling, Kentucky, a small town thirty-two miles east of Lexington and on the fringe of the coal mountains of eastern Kentucky. Since nobody on either side of my family had ever graduated from college, nothing much was expected of me. My father told me he was going to stop supporting me — "my lazy butt," as he put it — when I turned sixteen. But to give the devil his due, he also helped me get a summer job keeping score for the Northern and Central Little Leagues at Castlewood Park in Lexington.

That job paid me $3 per game, and one of my responsibilities was writing weekly summaries of each league's games that would be published in the Sunday edition of the *Lexington-Herald Leader*. I typed the stories on a manual typewriter at home, then rode my bicycle to the newspaper office to deliver them on Friday afternoons. Billy Thompson, the assistant sports editor of the *Herald*, took a liking to me and hired me to replace George Robinson, who was leaving for Centre College, as the Henry Clay High beat reporter. And so, in early August 1959, did my career begin, less than a month after my 16th birthday.

From that time until now, I was blessed to get jobs that gave me access to some of the most extraordinary people and events of my time. Working for either *Sports Illustrated* magazine or the *Courier-Journal* in Louisville, I typed out stories from forty-five states, Mexico, Canada, and France. I should mention here that I came to have a sort of dual personality. My byline was "Billy Reed" until I went to work for *SI* in 1968. The editors there, most of them Ivy League graduates, decided that "Billy" was "too colloquial," or something like that, so they insisted I change it to something more formal. Since I had never been called anything but "Billy," I didn't know what to do. I finally settled on "William F. Reed," and that was the byline that appeared on all my *SI* stories.

One time I remember proudly telling Bob Knight, the controversial basketball coach at Indiana University, that I got my degree in English from Transylvania College (now University) in 1966 and had never taken a journalism class. "Yeah," he said, "it shows." But while I was studying Shakespeare and Proust at Transy, I also was learning about writing on deadline and developing a style at the *Herald-Leader*. Both educations were equally important.

I fell in love with newspapers in 1958, the first time I timidly ventured into the *Herald-Leader* newsroom, which was on the third floor of a squatty yellow building on Short Street behind the courthouse. The sound and fury of the newsroom — the clacking typewriters, the ringing phones, the editors and reporters bustling here and there — was intoxicating. When I worked up the nerve to ask the location of the sports department, an editor wearing a visor with a cigarette between his lips, pointed upward. The sports department was on floor 3 ½, which was a huge metal platform attached to the ceiling by cables.

I couldn't believe it, but I climbed the stairs nonetheless. The platform was filled with people, desks, chairs, bookcases, and filing cabinets. How could cables be strong enough to support all that? I swear, the floor swayed when one of the heavyset editors lumbered across it. Still, this was the place where Billy Thompson typed out most of his popular "Pressbox Pickups" columns and where I would work with people like Mike Ruehling, David "Butch" Thompson, David Vance, Rick Bailey, David Hawpe, and Russ Shain, who remain friends to this day. The late Johnny McGill also was part of our group.

When I left Lexington for the *Courier* after graduating from Transy in 1966, I already had Billy Thompson's old job as assistant sports editor at the *Herald*. I turned down a raise to $112.50 a week to remain at the *Herald* because the *C-J* had offered me $150 a week. Said one of the *H-L* editors, "Don't worry . . . he'll be back." The guy turned out to be right, but it took twenty-one years and unusual circumstances to make it happen.

Now and then, I'll still take a stroll through a press box or a press room just to see if I know anybody. Long ago, you see, I swore I would not be that old guy taking up space reserved for the working press and boring the current generation of journalists with stories about the good ol' days. It has worked out fine. Most of my contemporaries are long gone, and the current dashing knights of the keyboard tend to speak a language that is unfamiliar to me. I never had to be bothered with tweeting and texting during games, and trust me, I'm quite happy about that.

I also don't miss the travel. My first airplane trip to cover a game came in 1965, when I accompanied the Eastern Kentucky University basketball team on a chartered DC-3 — that was a propeller plane, for heaven's sake — and I didn't stop until I got out of the daily newspaper business in 2001.

At first, traveling was glamorous. During my first full-time stint with *Sports Illustrated*, from 1968 through 1972, the magazine was making so much money that we often got to fly first class. I particularly remember a San Francisco-to-New York trip in the early '70s, when my first-class neighbors on a 747 were Debbie Reynolds, whose best acting days were behind her, and Dustin Hoffman, who was just coming into stardom. I tried to be cool about it. I didn't speak to either of them until we were at baggage claim, when I shook hands with Hoffman and told him how much I enjoyed *The Graduate* and *Midnight Cowboy*.

I looked it up once and found that I had written almost 800 pieces for *SI* from 1968 through 1998, the year I retired. That includes twelve cover stories, but it also includes a lot of less important stuff, like all the harness racing stories I did when *SI* covered that sport thoroughly because managing editor Andre Laguerre loved horse racing of all kinds. I knew I didn't have the talent of a Frank Deford, a Dan Jenkins, or a John Underwood, so I decided I'd make myself useful by being versatile. I wrote at least one *SI* story on fifteen different sports, including a "Point After" column in which my bashing of soccer brought all the soccer moms in North America out of the woodwork.

I loved *SI*, even did a piece for them in November 2017, but it was the *Courier-Journal* that was dearest to my heart. When I was there, from 1966 to '68 and again from 1972 to '86, the *C-J* consistently made *Time* magazine's list of the nation's top 10 newspapers and had one of the best sports sections in the nation. Before the Internet shrunk the world, we put out four editions every night and had home delivery in all 120 Kentucky counties and much of southern Indiana. Beyond that, we had influence in our circulation area that papers no longer enjoy.

The deadline for the four-star edition, which was sent by truck to the most distant parts of the state, was around 9 p.m. The deadline for the five-star, which went mainly to central Kentucky, was 11:10 p.m. It was midnight for the six-star, the Indiana edition, and 1 a.m. for the seven-star, the edition that went to Louisville and surrounding counties. Sometimes, in the case of a late-starting important game, we would change the deadlines to make sure it was in the readers' hands the next morning.

Lord, did I love it all, especially the incredible sense of teamwork among editors, reporters, photographers, and production people. I'll never forget the evening in 1974 when killer tornadoes struck Louisville and other parts of Kentucky. It was all hands on board that night, and I'll always remember the pride I felt when the last edition began rolling off the presses and we had done a prize-worthy job of covering one of the worst weather disasters in Louisville's history.

I'm not so sure that my best work didn't come after I left *Sports Illustrated* and New York City in 1972 to return to Louisville and the *Courier*. At first, I was an investigative reporter, and doggone if my friend Jim Bolus and I didn't do a series on fixed horse races that enabled us to win a major award over a couple of guys named Bernstein and Woodward, who then were in the midst of a little story named Watergate for the *Washington Post*.

Then, in 1974, when popular *C-J* general columnist Joe Creason died of a sudden heart attack, Carol Sutton, the first female managing editor of a major American paper, picked me to succeed him at age 31. I did that, writing about everything from Elvis Presley to moonshine, until 1977, when I was named to succeed the talented Dave Kindred as the *C-J*'s sports editor. Trust me, nobody should have to follow both Creason and Kindred in the same lifetime.

I remained sports editor until the end of 1986, less than six months after the Bingham family had sold all its first-class media properties (*C-J*, *Louisville Times*, WHAS radio and TV) to a variety of businesses who cared more about the bottom line than great reporting. I gave up my job — my dream job, actually — with enormous sadness because it had been a win-win deal. The paper allowed me to cover the major sporting events — the World Series, Super Bowl, NCAA Final Four, Triple Crown races, major golf tournaments, and big college football games — and I paid them back by writing five, six, even seven columns a week.

By the time I came back to the *H-L* in 1987, the paper had improved enough to compete with the *C-J* in central and eastern Kentucky. Black-and-white photography had been replaced by color, something the *C-J* didn't yet have, and the standards were much higher under the ownership of the Knight-Ridder chain and the leadership of a brilliant editor named John Carroll.

I also went back to full-time status at *SI* a year later and worked for both until 1998, when I ended my *SI* career with a cover story about LSU's football win over Florida. Three years later, *The Herald-Leader* and I parted company. From then until now, I've done a lot of things — books, government, politics, education, radio and TV, service on boards — and continued to write for various websites and publications.

Looking back, I was blessed throughout my career with an incredible series of friends, mentors, role models, and people who saw things in me that I didn't see in myself. They pushed me hard because they cared. I'm confident these sort of people are still out there to help disadvantaged kids, if only they can find each other.

I should say here that while I'm proud of my career, I also realize that many of my classmates from elementary school through college have made far greater contributions to society. I think of Dr. William H. Brooks, the accomplished neurosurgeon who has been one of my best friends since the eighth grade. Or classmates such as Larry Langan, Bill Poulson, Bruce Davis, Glen Bagby, Finbarr Saunders, Buddy Cowgill, Bob Nesmith, Bill and Stephanie Gardner, and many more who became lawyers, doctors, educators, business innovators, or government leaders.

Here is probably where I need to mention Mitch McConnell.

In the summer of 1956, when I turned thirteen, I was picked to play for the Giants of the Beechmont Pony League. We played our games at the Naval Ordnance Plant in Louisville's south end, and we had to work the wool uniforms that were way too big for us and hot as hell, besides. One of my teammates was Addison "Mitch" McConnell, whose family had moved to Louisville from Georgia. Although he had undergone a serious case of polio a few years earlier, Mitch both pitched and played shortstop and was one of our better players.

Yes, this is the same guy who was elected to the U.S. Senate from Kentucky in 1984 and eventually became Majority Leader, making him one of the four or five most powerful politicians in the nation. In fact, I met him through student government before we were baseball teammates. In the 1955-56 academic year, he was in the eighth grade at DuPont Manual and I was in the seventh. We each represented our classes on the executive board of the Student Council.

To say we went in radically different directions politically would be an understatement. So, when I tell the story about Mitch during speeches, I always say, "Some say the nation would have been much better off if I'd gone into politics and Mitch had become a sports writer."

Mitch would laugh at that. I think.

Chapter Two

INTRO TO WRITING 101

When I talk to journalism students, the first thing they usually ask is how much money I make. I always tell them that money should be the last consideration in picking your life's work. Find something that (a) you enjoy and (b) can do reasonably well. If you can do that, your chances of being happy are better than if you go into a field that you don't like but pays well.

Then the kids always want to know, "How do you learn to write?" Even now, I can only say there is no formula. Writing is not like math or science, where there are rules and paths to solving problems. The best way to learn to write is by doing it, over and again, every chance you get. Even then, you might not ever become the kind of writer you want to be if you don't have a certain knack for it.

The basis of all good writing is good reporting. The more facts and interviews you have, the better your chances of writing an interesting story. There's nothing glamorous about reporting. It's strictly a matter of hard work. And it's a truism that not every great reporter can become a great writer, but every great writer also is a great reporter.

Every successful writer I've ever known has been helped by a variety of mentors, some in journalism and some not. These are the people who want to see you succeed to the point that they're willing to push you and challenge you to see if you have the right stuff.

From 1959–66, I cut my teeth at the morning *Lexington Herald* and the afternoon *Leader*. Billy Thompson, the assistant sports editor of the *Lexington Herald*, gave me my first job and was my first role model. He had a unique way of writing his popular "Pressbox Pickups" column. On any given night, Billy would have no column when we began work at 4 p.m. But as the night wore on, people would call him with tips or bits of information. He wrote them and sent them to the composing room as they came in, and by the end of the evening, he would have a full notes column chock full of news and rumors.

At the *Leader*, I learned to write with the second-day approach. In other words, since the news was in the morning paper, we needed to put a fresh spin on it, so we featurized our news stories or spun them toward the future. Sports Editor Winfield Leathers was a stickler for grammar and accuracy, and his successor, Russell Rice, a former Marine, taught me about discipline and clarity. But it was Russell's assistant, Larry Van Hoose, who helped me more than anyone.

A native of Paintsville who loved golf almost as much as he did Republican politics, Larry worked diligently with me to break my bad habits and elevate my goals. When I asked Larry how to improve my writing, he told me to read the great Red Smith every chance I got. Red, then writing for the *New York Herald-Tribune* syndicate, wrote beautiful prose that sometimes approached poetry. Larry also told me that if I wanted to work with the best, I should aspire to someday working for *Sports Illustrated*, which was well on the way to becoming the best-written magazine in the world.

At the time, Larry was *SI*'s "stringer," or correspondent, in Lexington. He turned much of that responsibility over to me, which enabled me to pick up a few extra bucks and, more importantly, meet the magazine's writers and editors whenever they came through town.

Not all my mentors came from the newspaper business. C.M. Newton, the Transylvania College basketball coach, taught me that winning isn't important unless it's done the right way, and S.T. Roach, the basketball coach at all-black Dunbar High, taught me much about the importance of treating everybody with respect and dignity.

C.M. was responsible for me getting a college degree.

After graduating from Henry Clay, I was set to go to UK on a journalism scholarship. But my parents got divorced, and it was pretty nasty. I was left to help my mother and sisters while working full-time at the *Herald-Leader* and carrying a full load of classes at UK. I was 19.

Every day I had to be at work at 7, then go cross-town to UK, where finding a parking place was as challenging then as it is now. Then I would come back to the newspaper office for a couple of hours before going to cover a game or hang out with friends (sometimes we would even study).

It got to be so overwhelming and depressing that I was ready to quit school and spend the rest of my career at the newspaper. But when I told this to C.M., whom I had gotten to know by covering some of his Transylvania team's games, he said, "Don't quit. You need to get that degree. Come to Transy and I'll help you get some student aid. But whatever you do, don't quit."

I took his advice. The *Herald-Leader* building was only a couple of blocks from Transy's campus, easy walking distance. Besides that, the classes were so small that I got to know the professors, who all were willing to work with me when my newspaper job forced me to be late on an assignment. I became my family's first college graduate in August, 1966, and I've always given C.M. most of the credit. I wish every coach believed in education as much as he did.

At the *Courier-Journal* from 1966-68, I discovered how much more I had to learn. Earl Cox, then the administrative assistant to sports editor Earl Ruby, gave me more good assignments than a guy my age probably deserved, and I became friends with Dave Kindred, whom I've always regarded as the Red Smith of my generation. Like Red, Dave had a graceful way with words that was unique.

At *Sports Illustrated* from 1968 through 1972, my guardian angel was Jerry Tax, an assistant managing editor who, like me, had a special affinity for college basketball and horse racing. He, Roy Terrell, and Bob Ottum took me under their wing, and I learned much just from listening to great *SI* writers such as Dan Jenkins, Mark Kram, John Underwood, and Frank Deford talk about how they approached their work.

Kram was our lead boxing writer, and he never saw himself as a mere sports writer. He was a fireplug of a man who had blond hair and constantly puffed a pipe. One of his main claims to fame was getting into a fight with the novelist Norman Mailer at a cocktail party. But, jeez, could he write. I think he liked me, but I'm not sure because he was always pushing me to put more of myself in my stories, to experiment, and to take risks. It was good advice, and I worked on it.

Who was the best writer at *SI*? Well, I happened to be in the Ho-Ho Bar, next to the Time-Life Building, one Sunday night when Kram and Tex Maule, then the pro football writer and a favorite of managing editor Laguerre, got into a heated debate about just that. One of them eventually threw a glass at the other, and I figured that was a good time for me to go back to the office and help with some proof-reading.

The difference between magazine writing and newspaper writing has much to do with how you set up and develop a story. Magazine pieces are generally longer, which means you have more space to flex your verbs. The best magazine pieces examine a person or topic in far greater detail and context than can usually be found in newspapers. For example, I remember the first time I read "The Rabbit Hunter," Frank Deford's insightful profile of Indiana basketball coach Bob Knight. I thought I knew Knight pretty well, but Deford saw him in a way that could only make me think, "Damn, why didn't I see that?"

At all the Time, Inc., publications, the editors believed in "personal journalism," which mean they wanted you to put a lot of yourself into the stories. This is what Mark Kram was trying to tell me. But given my newspaper background, where I learned to keep my own feelings and opinions out of stories, this was a hard transition for me to make.

I suppose, at heart, I'm a newspaper stiff. I liked the challenge of writing on deadline. I liked the instant gratification of seeing my photo and byline the next morning. I liked the idea of writing the first draft of history.

So, how do you learn to write?

Red Smith once said that writing was easy. "All you have to do is open a vein and let it bleed," he said. To some, indeed, writing is a tortured experience. Every word in every sentence must be exactly right. At games, they're always the last to send in their stuff, feeling guilty if they didn't use every second available to them.

I was never like that. I enjoyed the experience of writing, especially writing fast on deadline. It was a challenge that I relished. Even at *SI*, deadlines were important. If, say, I were covering a Saturday night football game, I'd get back to my hotel room at midnight and begin typing on my Olivetti portable in order to have my copy into the New York office by 10 a.m. Sunday. If you were working in a small town, you hoped that somebody would be in the local Western Union office at that time to re-type your copy on a Teletype machine. The advent of computers meant we could transmit from our rooms, one of the positives about the technological revolution.

If you want to become a columnist or magazine writer, you must read the writers you admire and try to figure out how they do things. I attempted to emulate the best. I went through a Red Smith stage, a Jim Murray stage, a Jimmy Breslin stage. This is how you figure out what you can and can't do. Eventually, if you're fortunate, your own style and viewpoint will emerge. You will know it because you will feel comfortable with it. But you must remember that there's no such thing as a template for the perfect writer. Even the best ones do it differently.

Here are the tools I think are important.

The first thing to do is to master the fundamentals of grammar. When I was in school, we diagrammed sentences to understand how the various parts of speech related to each other. I don't know why our schools no longer teach students to diagram.

You must know and understand logic. The best stories have a certain flow to them in which facts are arranged in a way that's entertaining, informative, and easy for the reader to understand.

A good writer should always be trying to expand his or her vocabulary. Words are your tools, and you should aspire to learn as many as you can, so you can be as precise as possible in your descriptions of people, places, and things.

Write in a clear, concise way. At the *C-J*, they told us the average reader had an eighth-grade education. Short sentences and paragraphs are usually better than long, convoluted ones. It's essential to keep the reader engaged from beginning to end.

Make sure your facts are accurate. Even if you're expressing your opinion in a column, you must be able to support that opinion with facts. If you don't know your stuff, it will be obvious and nobody will want to read you.

Too many of today's writers use meaningless quotes instead of letting their senses come into play. Write about what you see, smell, and hear. Paint word pictures for your audience. And only use quotes that add substance to your story.

Try to write with a light touch instead of a heavy hand. The best writers entertain their readers as much as informing them. Remember that you are writing about games, not anything that's going to change the world.

Be observant. I was once interviewing Paul "Bear" Bryant, the iconic football coach at Alabama. I looked at his hands and noticed that he only wore one ring. When I asked him which of his national championship teams gave him that ring, he said, "None of 'em. It came from my first team at Texas A&M. Only won one game." That told me volumes about the things Bryant held dear.

Don't be timid. Have the courage to experiment. You'll never know how good you can be until you get outside your safety zone.

Sometimes, when you stumble into a good story, you just try to get out of the way and let the muse work. There's nothing worse than "overwriting." For example, I remember a 1980 football game in which Indiana defeated Kentucky at Commonwealth (now Kroger) Stadium. The winning touchdown pass was caught by Steve Corso, son of Hoosier coach Lee Corso, the same guy whom today's fans know for his zany antics on ESPN's College GameDay.

That was a good enough angle in itself. But there was more. The defensive back who got beat on the winning catch was Greg Mobley, who had just attended the funeral of his beloved grandmother in Middlesboro. So, one kid's moment of triumph compounded another's misery. I remember praying that I would just play it straight because this was one of the stories that needed no embellishment.

Sadly, I think the internet has negatively affected the quality of sports writing. If you were to ask me to name the best wordsmiths of today, about the only name I could give you is Pat Forde of Yahoo! Sports, a former columnist in Louisville. Mike Lupica is still a must-read in New York, and there may be others with whom I'm not familiar. But no sports writer today has the power and influence of the giants who wrote syndicated columns in the 1930s through the '90s.

Still, there always will be a place somewhere for a writer who can tell a story well. Movies and TV need scriptwriters, and corporate America needs top-drawer writers for its newsletters, magazines, and websites. Many of these jobs pay well, too, for you aspiring writers who are interested in such things.

After all the stories I've done over six decades, all I know for sure is that I have never written a perfect story. Some are better than others, sure, but a writer always can find that one little thing or two that he wished he or she had done differently or better.

Once Red Smith was asked why he wrote five columns a week instead of the three his competitors were doing. "Because if I write a bad one," Smith said, "there's always the next day to make up for it."

I suppose that's also the way I looked at it.

Chapter Three

STILL MY NATIONAL PASTIME

I've never been able to adequately describe to young people how big baseball was when I was growing up in the 1950s. Back then, the NFL and the NBA were in their formative years. Golf and tennis were considered to be pastimes for the rich folks. College football, boxing, and horse racing were popular, but nothing approached baseball.

There were only sixteen major-league franchises then, none west of the Mississippi River, but many cities and towns had minor-league franchises. The bottom rung on the ladder was Class D, and it went all the way up to Class AAA, which was just below the majors. Every week during the season, the *Sporting News*, considered baseball's "Bible," was filled with news and box scores that youngsters like me studied far more diligently that we did our schoolwork.

My grandparents in Mt. Sterling subscribed to one of the Cincinnati papers, and at the start of spring training, I always looked for the edition that had a photo of the writers and columnists covering the Reds in Tampa, Florida. I memorized their names: Pat Harmon, Lou Smith, Earl Lawson, Jim Ferguson, Si Burick, Ritter Collett, and a few others. I could imagine no job in the world better than covering spring training for a newspaper.

I was born and bred a Reds fan, but I followed the big leagues in their entirety, along with the Louisville Colonels of the American Association, the top farm team of the Boston Red Sox from the 1930s to the late '60s. Pee Wee Reese played for the Colonels before the Red Sox, who owned his contract, traded him to the Brooklyn Dodgers, where he became shortstop and captain of the "Boys of Summer" teams immortalized by author Roger Kahn.

In those early days of black-and-white TV, I hustled home from school to catch the final innings of the World Series, which always seemed to match the New York Yankees against the Dodgers. I was a Dodgers' fan, mainly because of Pee Wee, but also because of their diversity. The Dodgers had Jackie Robinson, who broke baseball's color barrier in 1947, and three other African-American stars — catcher Roy Campanella, infielder Jim "Junior" Gilliam, and pitching ace Don Newcombe. They also had an Italian-American right fielder named Carl Furillo and a Hispanic outfielder named Sandy Amoros to go with white stars Reese, first-baseman Gil Hodges, third-baseman Billy Cox, center fielder Duke Snider, and pitchers such as Carl Erskine, Johnny Podres, Preacher Roe, and Clem Labine.

I was watching on TV in 1955 when the Dodgers finally prevailed behind Podres in the final game. The final out of the game was a grounder to Reese, and as Pee Wee told me years later, "I was afraid I wouldn't get it to Hodges in time to get the runner. That throw seemed to take forever."

Like most of America, I was stunned after the 1957 season when owners Walter O'Malley of the Dodgers and Horace Stoneham of the New York Giants moved their franchises to Los Angeles and San Francisco, respectively. I was more upset by that than the news that the Russians had beaten the U.S. to outer space, launching Sputnik on Oct. 4, 1957.

In the summer of 1960, I belonged to a group that was selected to represent Henry Clay (High School) at an International Key Club convention in Boston. I checked the Red Sox schedule and saw that the team would be at home while I was there, so I asked Billy Thompson if he could get me some Red Sox tickets. He came though, bless his heart, which meant that I got to see the immortal Ted Williams play in Fenway Park during his last season with the Red Sox. (Aspiring journalists should make it a point to read John Updike's class piece on Williams' last game in Fenway. Wonderful stuff.)

Besides being one of the best hitters in baseball history, Williams was more than just a sports hero. He joined the Navy and flew combat flights during World War II. Then, during the Korean War, he went on active duty again and flew jets. The only negative about him, at least from a young sports writer's perspective, was that he had only contempt for the press, especially the scribes who covered him in Boston.

The winter after Williams' retirement, the *Herald-Leader* sports department got a call from former baseball commissioner A.B. "Happy" Chandler, who was most respected — or reviled, as the case may be — for defying his bosses, the big-league owners, and approving Jackie

Robinson's contract with the Brooklyn Dodgers in 1946. The owners had voted 15 to 1 against letting Robinson play, but Chandler ignored them. "I figured I'd meet my maker someday," he liked to say, "and when He asked me why I didn't let the boy play, I think 'the color of his skin' would be an insufficient answer."

Chandler also had been known as the "players' commissioner" because he sided with their fight to get better working conditions. One of his admirers was Ted Williams, so Chandler wanted the newspaper to know that he was having lunch with Williams at the Idle Hour Country Club in Lexington and that Ted had consented to an interview.

As I recall it, none of the older guys in the department wanted to go because they knew how Williams felt about the media. But I had no such qualms. I figured no matter what happened, I'd at least be able to say I met the great man. So, I showed up at Idle Hour just as Chandler and Williams were finishing lunch, notebook in hand and heart in my throat.

Well, Williams couldn't have been more pleasant. Maybe it was because he could see I was just a star-gazing kid who had no axe to grind. Maybe he was just trying to do Chandler a favor. Whatever, he answered my questions fully and graciously.

When I switched from the morning *Herald* to the afternoon *Leader* in the summer of 1961, it opened the way for me to cover the Reds because Winfield Leathers, the sports editor, didn't care much for baseball. So, I wrote a lot of Reds stuff as they surprised the baseball world by winning the National League pennant and earning a World Series berth opposite — of course! — the Yankees. This was the year that Roger Maris had hit 61 home runs to beat the record of 60 set by Babe Ruth in 1927, but his feat was accompanied in the record books by an asterisk because baseball had expanded the season from the 154 games played in Ruth's time to 162.

Much to my surprise and delight, Leathers applied for a World Series credential in my name and baseball approved it. So, I covered games three and four in Crosley Field but had to miss the fifth game because I didn't want to miss class at UK. The Yanks won to complete a 4–1 Series victory.

At the time I covered these games, I was less than three months past my 18th birthday. So, I've always claimed to be the youngest writer ever credentialed to cover a World Series game for a major newspaper. That's my story, and I'm sticking to it until somebody corrects me.

I saw Mickey Mantle play in that World Series, and I got to meet him five years later in a situation that was unique for the time and utterly unthinkable today.

In the summer of 1966, after my graduation from Transylvania, my buddy Larry Langan and I drove to New York City, so I could have my first interview with *Sports Illustrated*. We stayed at a hotel near Times Square in a room so small that the 6-foot-5 Langan could stand in the middle of the room and literally touch the opposite walls.

By covering Morehead State games for the *Herald-Leader*, I had become friends with Steve Hamilton, a pitcher for the Yankees who had been a basketball star for Morehead in the late 1950s. "Billy, if you ever get to New York," Steve told me, "give me a call, and I'll get you some tickets to a Yankees' game."

So from our little hotel room, I dialed Yankee Stadium and asked for the clubhouse. Next thing I knew, I was talking to somebody I thought was a clubhouse boy. When I asked for Steve, he said, "He's not here now — anything I can do for you?" I told him my story, and he said, "Well, this is Mickey Mantle, and there will be two tickets in my box waiting for you at Will Call tomorrow."

When I hung up and told Langan what had happened, he began laughing. "You idiot," he said. "That wasn't Mickey Mantle. That was somebody pulling your leg." And he continued to rag on me the rest of the day.

Nevertheless, we got up the next day and took the subway to Yankee Stadium. I walked up to Will Call and asked for two tickets in my name. And there they were, just as the voice on the phone had promised. Now it was my turn to do the razzing.

Soon as we sat down in Mantle's box, Hamilton popped out of the dugout. I got his attention and told him my story. "OK," he said, "meet me right here after the game, and I'll take you into the locker room and introduce you to Mickey, so you can thank him."

And that's exactly what happened. We spent about fifteen minutes talking with him, and I noticed that his bad legs were wrapped tightly and he seemed to move gingerly. But as was the case with Ted Williams, he was kind and gracious.

Many years later, I met Mantle again at a dinner thrown by A. Ray Smith, owner of the Louisville Redbirds. The ravages of alcohol were taking their toll, but he still was sharp as he exchanged quips with Pee Wee Reese about the Dodgers-Yankees rivalry in the World Series.

At a similar A. Ray production, I also met Mantle's predecessor in center field for the Yankees, the great Joe DiMaggio. Going into the interview, A. Ray had only one admonition for me: "Don't ask him anything about Marilyn." That would be the sex goddess Marilyn Monroe, to whom DiMaggio had a brief and torrid marriage after his retirement.

After covering the 1961 World Series for the *Lexington Leader*, I didn't get credentialed again until 1977, the same year I became sports editor of the *C-J*. I covered it every year from then until 1986, when poor first-baseman Bill Buckner of the Red Sox let a ground ball go through his legs in Game 6. That took the starch out of Boston, which lost that game and the next to let the New York Mets steal a Series that seemed to have Boston's name on it.

During that time, the Louisville Redbirds' parent team, the St. Louis Cardinals, made the World Series in both 1982, the first year the Redbirds were in Louisville, and 1985. I enjoyed those two because I had come to know some of the Cardinals' players in Louisville. I also knew the writers and broadcasters who covered St. Louis, so I almost felt like a part of the home team.

Sometime after the NFL merged with the AFL and held its first Super Bowl in 1967, pro football surpassed baseball as the "National Pastime." Perhaps it was inevitable, given America's fascination with violence and need for instant gratification, but I hated to see it. Baseball has never really lost me, although I was plenty angry when the game let a labor dispute between players and owners cancel the 1994 World Series.

There's much I don't like about how the game has evolved. I don't like all the wasted time between pitches, the pitching-by-committee system, the overabundance of strikeouts because everyone is swinging from the heels, and the lack of attention to fundamentals such as bunting, hitting the cutoff man, etc.

Still, I much prefer baseball to the NFL or the NBA. Maybe it's just something that's in my DNA. As a kid, I collected baseball cards and played sandlot ball every day the sun shone. Baseball taught me as much about math and geography as my school classes. And a trip to Crosley Field, usually for a Sunday double-header, was the highlight of any summer.

I still keep score every time I go to a Louisville Bats or Reds game. I taught my daughters Amy and Susan that fine art, but I'm sure they've long since forgotten. I still like afternoon games better than night ones, but there's no bad time to be at a ball park, especially when it's warm and you're surrounded by the sweet sounds of summer.

One more baseball story.

Since pro baseball returned to Louisville in 1982, both the Reds and Bats have had some good managers. My favorite remains Jim Fregosi, a former All-Star shortstop with the California Angels who managed the Redbirds in 1984 and '85 before getting the Chicago White Sox job.

Fregosi had a bit of a chip on his shoulder when he came to town. In his mind, he was a big-league guy operating in a bush-league market. At times, he was brusque and curt with the local media, whose collective baseball knowledge he obviously didn't respect.

But A. Ray Smith wanted Fregosi and I to be friends, and so we were. One night after a game, as we were nursing beers at the bar where Fregosi's future wife Joni worked, we fell into a conversation about the media.

"Jim, dealing with the media should be the easiest part of your job," I told him. "Most of them are inclined to be hero-worshippers, so just a little bit of kindness on your part will go a long way. Why should you care what anybody writes or says on the radio? Just do your job and everything else will fall into place."

Fast-forward now to 1993, when Fregosi was in the World Series as manager of the Philadelphia Phillies. I was sitting in the *Herald-Leader* sports department when one of the editors came up to me with an Associated Press story and said, "You're mentioned in here."

I couldn't imagine why that would be, but sure enough, Fregosi had mentioned me in an interview. "Everything I know about the media," he said, "I learned from Billy Reed in Louisville." Well, I seriously doubt that. Still, it was nice of Jim to send me a shout-out from the World Series.

Chapter Four

A STUDY IN BLACK AND WHITE

O ne night many years ago, I was having dinner with a bunch of sports writers in Birmingham when the subject of race came up. The group included David Housel, then the sports information director at Auburn, a heavyset man who would be a finalist in any Mr. Nice Guy contest. A native of Alabama, David loves his state and Auburn, his alma mater. He didn't say much during the dinner conversation, mostly just listened, but when we were done, he grabbed a couple of us and said, "Come with me, I want to show you something."

He drove us to the 16th Street Baptist Church, the same place where Ku Klux Klan bombs killed four young black girls on a Sunday morning in 1963. As he talked about it, he began crying, his wide shoulders quivering. He wasn't doing it for show. The tears were coming from his heart. This wonderful son of Alabama was telling us how hurt he was that such a tragedy could happen in his beloved state.

David and I are roughly the same age, so I'm sure we had a lot of the same experiences growing up. When I began following sports in the early 1950s, the first African-American stars were beginning to change things forever. I read everything I could about Hank Aaron (of Mobile, Alabama), Willie Mays, Jackie Robinson, and many others, often with the revolutionary music of Chuck Berry, Little Richard, or Bo Diddley playing in the background.

Even at a young age, I couldn't understand why the same people we idolized as entertainers could not eat at the same lunch counter or drink from the same water fountains that we did. I remember a trip to visit family members in Birmingham, where white and "colored" had different facilities. But I didn't dwell on it much because everybody, including the African-Americans, seemed to accept it as just the way things were.

But then Rosa Parks refused to give up her seat on that bus in Montgomery and Emmett Till was brutally murdered at age fourteen in Mississippi, and suddenly everything began changing rapidly, even though the states from the Old South fought it bitterly in what amounted almost to a second Civil War. But most Americans could not ignore the images brought into their homes every night by the new phenomenon of TV.

When I moved to the *Lexington Leader* in 1961 and was put on the high school beat, Lexington's high schools were still segregated, although it had been seven years since the landmark Brown v. Board of Education case that struck down segregation in public schools. There were five all-white schools (Henry Clay, Lafayette, Bryan Station, Lexington Catholic, and University High) and two black ones (Dunbar and Douglass).

By this time, Dunbar, coached by S.T. Roach, had supplanted Lafayette and Henry Clay as the best program in the city. Nevertheless, the morning and afternoon papers, which did not employee any blacks in the news and editorial departments, did not send reporters to staff the Dunbar games, relying instead on "correspondents" to telephone in the results. The news departments were just as prejudiced. The *Leader* employed a black woman named Helen Berryman to do a weekly column entitled "Colored Notes & Obituaries" to keep the black community separated.

At my callow age, I was by no means a Civil Rights crusader. But I did believe that the best team in the county deserved at least equal coverage with the others. So, I began showing up at some Dunbar games, which was a bigger deal to the black community than I realized at the time. In a different way, it also was a big deal to some of the editors at the *Herald-Leader*. I especially remember the time I ran into the city editor of one of the papers as I came into the office after covering a game.

"What game did you cover tonight?" he asked.

"Dunbar and Louisville Male," I said.

"What are you," he asked, "some kind of nigger lover?"

"No, sir," I said. "It was just the best game in town."

In truth, I did come to love Dunbar. The bigots had told me that black teams were undisciplined and couldn't handle pressure. The truth was exactly the opposite. Mr. Roach, as I always called him, demanded discipline and hard work as much as any coach I was ever around. He also demanded that his players respond to racist epithets by putting points on the scoreboard instead of opening their mouths.

Known as the "Bearcats," Dunbar wore green-and-white uniforms. After wins, their cheerleaders would chant, "The Bearcats did it again . . . the Bearcats did it again. . . ." I can still see George Wilson, wearing a huge brace on one knee, outjumping players much taller than his 6-foot-3. . . . Bobby Washington and Joe Hamilton, as fine a guard tandem as a high school team has ever had, penetrating or lighting it up from the outside. . . . Henry Davis casting a menacing glower at anybody trying to guard him.

I've always been proud of C.M. Newton, my mentor from Transylvania days, for doing more than anybody to integrate basketball in the South.

During most of his fifteen-year career at Transylvania, Newton had worked for a president named Dr. Frank Rose, who left Lexington to become president at the University of Alabama. When Alabama began looking for a new head basketball coach in 1968, Rose recommended Newton to Paul "Bear" Bryant, the Crimson Tide's football coach and athletics director. Bryant remembered Newton as one of Rupp's basketball players when Bryant was the UK football coach, so he invited him to Tuscaloosa to talk about the job.

At the time of their meeting, Perry Wallace of Vanderbilt, the first African-American to play hoops in the SEC, had just completed his sophomore season. Newton knew that Auburn had just signed a black player named Henry Harris, so he asked Bryant, "Will there be any restrictions on recruiting?" Bryant knew what he meant and told him that he would be free to recruit whomever he wanted, provided the players could do the academic work.

With the help of assistant Charles "Jock" Sutherland, a successful Kentucky high school coach who had joined the Alabama staff, Wendell Hudson became Alabama's first scholarship athlete after Newton's first season in Tuscaloosa. The historic event happened less than six years after then-Governor George Wallace had made his "stand in the schoolhouse door" (which actually was Foster Auditorium, where the Tide played basketball) and tried to stop the university's first black students by declaring "Segregation then, segregation now, segregation forever."

In the fall of 1972, Newton was well on his way to putting the Southeastern Conference's first all-black starting lineup on the floor. I called to tell him I wanted to come to Tuscaloosa and do a series for *The Courier-Journal* about what he was doing. Initially, he tried to discourage me because he was concerned about a backlash. The offices of the state chapter of the Ku Klux Klan were located at the opposite end of University Avenue from the campus.

But C.M. eventually relented because he trusted me to handle the story in a tasteful and non-inflammatory manner. So, I went to Tuscaloosa and met Leon Douglas, Charles Cleveland, T.R. Dunn, and the other black players who were turning Alabama into a national power in basketball. In the 1976 NCAA Mideast Regional, Alabama had unbeaten, top-ranked Indiana on the ropes late in the game, only to lose the 6-foot-10 Douglas on a controversial foul that pretty much decided the game in IU's favor.

In 1984, John Thompson of Georgetown became the first African American coach to win the NCAA championship. It was a landmark in the sport's history, but the prickly Thompson didn't like to talk about. He said he just wanted to be judged as a basketball coach, not as a racial pioneer. He also was a stickler about academics, which he felt was the most important benefit to playing college athletics.

As more and more money poured into sports from TV, the shoe companies, and Madison Avenue, many African American coaches and athletes stopped talking about race because, as Michael Jordan famously said, "Republicans buy sneakers, too." In other words, they didn't want to jeopardize their endorsement deals by saying anything that would anger White America.

So, it was a surprise in 2016 when Colin Kaepernick, then a quarterback with the San Francisco 49ers, took a knee during the playing of the national anthem to protest the inordinate number of blacks being killed by what he regarded as trigger-happy police. He made a valid point but drew so much attention for choosing the forum he did that his point was lost in the media frenzy.

The next season Kaepernick was a man without a team. Some say it was because he was washed up, but others contended the owners conspired against him. But the controversy was dying out until President Donald Trump breathed new life into it by changing the narrative. He ignored what Kaepernick was originally protesting and twisted it into a lack of respect for the flag and the military. It was a cynical trick, unworthy of anybody, much less the President, but Trump rallied his base against a black man who was only using his forum to raise a legitimate social issue.

This time a lot of athletes and entertainers stepped up to support Kaepernick's constitutional right of freedom of expression. But the owner of the Dallas Cowboys, Jerry Jones, finally threatened his players, saying that anybody who took a knee during the anthem would not play for his team. None of the Cowboys challenged him. America's team, indeed.

Nevertheless, I still believe that any time blacks and whites play on the same team — whether it's in the armed forces or the sports world or a business enterprise — it promotes mutual respect, greater understanding, and a special kind of brotherhood (or sisterhood, as the case may be). Just by being together every day and sharing the good, as well as the bad, bonds are forged that will last a lifetime.

I see it every time I go to a team reunion. Blacks and whites are genuinely glad to see each other. They love to laugh and tell stories about their playing days. They ask about each other's families and jobs. If only everybody could have that experience, I don't think our society would have Neo-Nazis, the Ku Klux Klan, or white supremacist groups.

The 1966 NCAA championship game between all-white Kentucky and Texas Western's all-black starting five now is widely accepted as what writer David Israel called "the Brown versus Board of Education of College Basketball." Just as widely accepted is *SI* writer Curry Kirkpatrick's story marking the 25th anniversary of the game, in which UK Coach Adolph Rupp is portrayed as a racist of Bull Connor dimensions.

The Kirkpatrick take is pure garbage. It's a fact that Rupp tried to integrate his program before any coach in the SEC or ACC. He offered 6-foot-6 Westley Unseld of Louisville Seneca High a scholarship in the spring of 1964 and tried to get Butch Beard of Breckenridge County a year later. Both went to Louisville not so much because they disliked Rupp but because of what was happening to blacks in the Deep South in those days.

As for the UK-Texas Western game, it's not as big, in my opinion, as what happened in the 1963 NCAA tournament. In those days, only the conference champions got an automatic bid to the NCAA tournament. Three times from 1959 through 1962, that bid would have gone to Mississippi State. But each time the team was forced to decline because the Mississippi legislature had an unofficial policy that no state school could play against teams with African-American players.

That rankled coach Babe McCarthy, who wanted to show that his team could compete against anybody in the nation. So, in 1963, when Mississippi State again got the SEC's automatic bid, McCarthy accepted, leading Gov. Ross Barnett to get a court injunction to stop the team from leaving the state. But the state police couldn't serve the warrant because the team was gone, spirited out of Starkville literally in the dark of night and taken to Nashville, where it caught a flight to the NCAA Mideast Tournament Site in East Lansing, Michigan.

On March 15, 1963, with Barnett and most others in Mississippi fuming, the Bulldogs met Loyola of Chicago, which had four black starters. When Joe Dan Gold, the Bulldogs' white captain, shook hands with Jerry Harkness, Loyola's black captain, it was, indeed, the moment when the college basketball world tilted.

Loyola won the game, 61-51, and went on to win the NCAA championship in Louisville's Freedom Hall, ruining Cincinnati's bid for a three-peat. But I would make the argument that the biggest winners in the tournament were Mississippi, college basketball, and the entire nation.

Chapter Five

THE SPORT OF
KINGS (AND WRITERS)

I n the spring of 1964, I got some of the best advice I ever received
from J.B. Faulconer, then the public-relations director at Keeneland.
Tall and ruggedly handsome, J.B. had the bearing of a military general,
which he was. At the time, he was second in command of the 100th
Division, U.S. Army Reserve.

I had first heard of him back in the 1950s, when he was a radio play-
by-play announcer for University of Kentucky games on the Ashland
Oil Network. I respected him immensely, so he had my complete attention when he pulled me aside one day in the Keeneland press box.

"Billy, if you're going to be a sports writer in Kentucky," he said, "you
have to know and write about Thoroughbred racing."

He then introduced me to Joe Hirsch, the executive columnist of
the *Daily Racing Form* and suggested I follow Joe a couple of mornings to learn the sport, meet its people, and become fluent in its arcane
language.

Hirsch was a tall New Yorker who was never without his trademark
dark aviator's glasses and a trench coat that could have come straight
from the CIA. In the mornings leading up to the Kentucky Derby, he
worked the barn area at Keeneland and other tracks like a ghost, slip-
ping in and out of trainers' offices to get the latest tidbits of information.

A kind and generous man, Joe taught me the importance of contacts.
Everybody on the backside of every track in America liked and trusted
Joe, and he never betrayed a confidence. If that meant not printing a
story that might be embarrassing to somebody in the industry, so be
it. As my friend Jim Bolus once said, "I'd just like to see the stories that
go into Joe's trash can."

But Joe's special relationship with the industry meant that he always
was ahead of the pack in covering the Derby and other major races.

Bolus, himself an extraordinary reporter, always said that he measured his Derby coverage by how well he was able to keep up with Hirsch's popular "Derby Doings" column in the *Racing Form*, known as the sport's "Bible."

Later that spring, I got my first opportunity to test how much I had learned from Joe. The racing editor at Lexington's afternoon paper, the *Leader*, was a pipe-smoking lawyer named Kent Hollingsworth. A brilliant writer, Hollingsworth also did not suffer fools gladly, and he wielded his sarcasm like a rapier. In order to escape his ridicule, I gave him a wide berth. But one day he came up to me and did me a great favor.

That year's Derby favorite was Northern Dancer, a Canadian-bred colt owned by E.P. Taylor of Toronto. His final Derby prep race was the Blue Grass Stakes at Keeneland, and the *Toronto Star* had called Hollingsworth to see if he could cover it for them. However, he was so busy that he asked if he could pass the assignment off to me. I think the pay was $25, big money for a college kid working his way through school.

Well, Northern Dancer easily won the first Thoroughbred race I ever covered, but that presented another problem: Jockey Bill Hartack was refusing to talk to the media unless he was paid. So, I went to Jimmy Nichols, who had ridden the second-place Allen Adair, to get his impressions of the winner. I typed up my story in the press box and took it to Western Union to send to Toronto, but also kept a carbon copy to run in the next afternoon's *Leader*.

As I look back, I'm proud of the fact that I was the first — and still the only — sports editor of the *Courier-Journal* to cover the sport on a year-round basis. My predecessors covered the Derby, of course, and sometimes they might even have covered a Derby prep race or two. But they didn't always go to Baltimore for the second jewel of racing's Triple Crown, the Preakness. And if they made it to Belmont Park on Long Island for the third jewel, it was often the last horse racing column they would write until the next spring.

But J.B. Faulconer had convinced me that nothing was more important to Kentucky than its horse industry. So, every year, besides covering the Triple Crown and the races leading up to it, I tried to spend a week at Saratoga in August, write about the fall meets at both Keeneland and Churchill Downs, and cover at least one of the big fall stakes in New York.

I loved Saratoga. It was, and still is, a stroll back in time, back to the days when race meetings had a carnival atmosphere. The lovely little town in upstate New York comes alive at dawn, when the workouts are being conducted at the race track. Then it's time for breakfast at Mother Goldsmith's or one of the other watch-pocket restaurants downtown.

The afternoon races always are entertaining because the best owners and trainers in America bring their stables to Saratoga. Then, in the evening, there's dinner at quaint places like The Wishing Well, where the tomatoes always are fresh. I remember an evening when my friend Mike Barry was presiding at The Wishing Well's piano bar. When he finally got tired of belting out show tunes and World War II standards, he announced he was leaving and began to get up from the piano stool.

But the former Betsy Hatfield of Lexington, ordinarily a lady of infinite class and charm, put her hand on his shoulder, slammed him back down, and said, "You're not going anywhere!" And he didn't until the former Miss Hatfield had to visit the ladies' room, at which time he grabbed his wife, Bennie, and made a quick move out the door.

I guess I loved racing so much because it's a writer's sport. It's impossible to spend much time on the backstretch at any track without running into a terrific human interest story. It might come from a groom, or it might come from a movie star or an Arab oil sheikh. But it always involves horses, and Americans are suckers for animals.

One of my favorite stories came at the 1977 Belmont Stakes, when Seattle Slew was bidding to become the first colt to win the Triple Crown while still unbeaten.

A couple of hours before post time, I went to Slew's barn to hang around with trainer Billy Turner, who had become a good friend. I met him that spring in Esposito's Tavern, the little joint across from Belmont's back stable gate that Turner called "my office." The tavern was run by brothers John and Junior Esposito, and it catered mostly to trainers, grooms, jockeys, and the media.

When the backstretch public-address system crackled with the first announcement that it was time for the Belmont trainers to bring their horses to the paddock, Turner kept Slew in his stall. He waited until I finally began to get nervous.

"Billy," I said, "don't you think it's time to take him over?"

"You don't think they're going to start without us, do you?" asked Billy, laughing and rubbing his hands together.

Billy knew that Slew was high-strung and didn't want him to spend much time in the chaos of the paddock. So, he got him there at the last possible moment, threw a saddle on his back, and gave a leg up to jockey Jean Cruguet, who headed straight for the track.

While the other owners and trainers headed for their seats in the clubhouse, Billy veered off into the grandstand area, and I followed. We found a place on the rail, amid the $2 bettors, and Billy asked if I would get him a vodka-and-tonic. This required me pushing to the front of the line in a grandstand bar, normally an act of suicide in New York, but I managed to get the drink and give it to Billy just before the starting gate broke open.

From where we stood, Turner couldn't see the action on the backstretch. But I had a pair of binoculars, so I did the best I could to call the race for him. "Billy, he's on the lead. . . . He's running smoothly. . . . Nothing is coming at him. . . . " As soon as Slew hit the finish line, Billy vaulted over the fence onto the track, where a Pinkerton tried to stop him until Turner convinced him that he was, indeed, the trainer of the unbeaten Triple Crown winner.

I loved Slew. During the 1978 World Series between the Yankees and Dodgers, I even skipped the Saturday afternoon game in Yankee Stadium, so I could cover the Jockey Club Gold Cup at Belmont Park. "Reed," said my friend Dave Kindred, "you're crazy." I begged to disagree. After all, the field for the Jockey Club Gold Cup included two Triple Crown winners: Seattle Slew and Affirmed. I wasn't going to miss that, and the heck with Reggie Jackson.

Unfortunately, the anticipated duel of the Triple Crown winners fell apart early. Shortly after Affirmed had left the starting gate, his saddle slipped, taking him out of contention. But that only opened the way for one of the greatest races I ever saw. Running easily on the lead, Seattle Slew appeared to be an easy winner until a horse named Exceller, ridden by Bill Shoemaker, came rolling out of the mist on a gray and rainy day to take the lead in the stretch.

But Slew fought back, regaining the lead, and battled Exceller the rest of the way before losing by a nose. I gave all due credit to the winner, but I also respected Seattle Slew as much in this defeat as I did in any of his victories. He had that indefinable something known as class, and as a breeding stallion, he passed on the trait to many of his sons and daughters.

I also was at Belmont in 1979 when Affirmed, now a 4-year-old, met Spectacular Bid, the wondrous gray colt who had missed the Triple Crown only because of a safety pin in a hoof and a bad ride by jockey Ron Franklin in the Belmont. Despite that bump in the road, Bid looked to be a 'freak," the racing term for a horse of singular ability.

Before the race, Grover G. "Bud" Delp, the cocky and loquacious man who trained Bid for the Meyerhoff family of Baltimore, predicted repeatedly that Bid would beat Affirmed handily. His counterpart, Laz Barrera, didn't respond but seethed in private over Delp's boasting. It turned out to be Affirmed's day, and I was there to see Barrera wag his finger at the owners and say, "They no mess with us." I liked and admired Laz, even though he always got Jim Bolus and I mixed up because we were together so often.

One of my best trainer friends was Woody Stephens, who accomplished a feat that I don't believe will ever be surpassed.

From 1982 through 1986, Woody won the Belmont Stakes five consecutive years. He did it with favorites and underdogs. He did it on fast tracks and in the slop. For the record, his winners were Conquistador Cielo (1982), Caveat (1983), Swale (1984), Crème Fraiche (1985), and Danzig's Connection (1986). In honor of the achievement, the New York Racing Association gave Woody a wristwatch. "Look at that, Bill," Woody would say to me. "Lukas ain't never gonna get one of them." He loved to beat D. Wayne Lukas.

Understanding that my affinity for the sport was not limited to the Derby, breeder John Gaines called me one day in the spring of 1982 to invite me to be his guest at the "They're Off" luncheon, which always was held the Friday before Churchill Downs opened its spring meet. He said he was the guest speaker and was going to announce something he thought would interest me.

Like J.B. Faulconer, Gaines was the sort of man who commanded attention and respect. He was an heir to the Gaines Dog Food fortune and used his wealth to become a patron of both Thoroughbred racing and the arts. If he said he had an idea, you could bet it was a good one. So, I showed up at the luncheon and was happy to see that Joe Hirsch was the only other racing writer there. His presence meant that something big was going to be announced.

And so did the world first hear about what became known as the Breeders' Cup. Gaines didn't call it that at the time. But he talked about having one day of championship racing in the late fall that would give the public reason to follow the sport after the Triple Crown. He saw it as racing's answer to the World Series or the Super Bowl. The event would be held at a different track every year and would be nationally televised. Five races would each have a $1 million purse, the Distaff for fillies would be run for $2 million, and The Classic, a mile-and-a-quarter event for 3-year-olds and up, would be the world's richest race with a purse of $3 million.

Most importantly, Gaines said he had the support of his fellow breeders, who would put .p the purse money along with corporate partners. The sport was so far-flung and fragmented that it was difficult to get a consensus on anything. But Gaines apparently had used logic and reason to get it done.

My story about the announcement was stripped across the top of the *C-J's* Metro section on Saturday morning. When I arrived at the press box that day, I was approached by Andy Beyer, the professorial turf writer for the *Washington Post* and inventor of the "Beyer Speed Figures" handicapping system.

"I read your piece today," said Beyer, "and I just wanted to tell you why it will never work."

Well, the first Breeders' Cup program was held in the late fall of 1984 at Hollywood Park. The inaugural Classic was won by the longshot Wild Again, ridden expertly by Pat Day. It was the win that moved Day from a regional jockey into a national star. More importantly, by any measurement, the Breeders' Cup was a huge success that reached all of Gaines' goals, at least to some extent.

Thanks to the Breeders' Cup, the racing world got to see the 1988 Distaff that included Winning Colors, the big gray who earlier that year had become the third filly ever to win the Kentucky Derby; Personal Ensign, who was 12-0 lifetime and trying to become the first major Thoroughbred to retire unbeaten; and Goodbye Halo, the winner of that year's Kentucky Oaks and a couple of other major races for 3-year-old fillies.

As expected, Winning Colors went straight to the lead, but Personal Ensign got hopelessly trapped in traffic. By the time jockey Randy Romero found some running room for Personal Ensign, Winning Colors was far in front. But Personal Ensign launched one of the greatest sustained runs ever seen and nipped the Derby winner in the final stride to retire 13-0. Goodbye Halo was third.

When the Breeders' Cup finally came home to Keeneland in 2015, long after John Gaines' death, I was there to see American Pharoah, who earlier that year had become the first Triple Crown winner since Affirmed, end his career with an impressive win in the Classic.

For me, it was a matter of coming full circle. I had covered my first race at Keeneland in 1964, and now here was the magnificent American Pharoah, electrifying the huge crowd and showing the world the sport at its finest, just as John Gaines had dreamed more than thirty years earlier.

Pharoah was trained by Bob Baffert, the best trainer in the sport's history. The Triple Crown was the last piece in a résumé that has no holes. When I first met Baffert in 1996, he seemed more interested in having a good time than becoming a legend. He and his buddy Mike Pegram liked Coors Light Beer so much that they named a filly Silverbulletday. All she did was blow away her competition in the 1999 Kentucky Oaks and Black-Eyed Susan, earning her a shot against the colts in the Belmont Stakes. After she set the early pace, the Belmont's mile-and-a-half caught up with her, and she finished ninth.

Like Lukas and Stephens, Baffert was a great ambassador for the sport. Young fans loved his quick wit, his non-conventional look: white hair, tinted glasses, jeans. He also discussed the arcane sport in a language anybody could understand. He and American Pharoah were the perfect tandem to give a new generation of racing fans their own Triple Crown winner.

Chapter Six

THE CHIPMUNKS

When I got into the newspaper business in 1959, sports was what Red Smith once called "the toy department." At least, that's how the editors and reporters on the news side seemed to view us. We were just overgrown kids, not real reporters. The condescension was as real as a Royal typewriter.

Sadly, we deserved it, for the most part. Sports writers and the people they covered tended to be friends, often drinking buddies. Investigative reporting was something the news side did. We rarely criticized poor performance and had an unwritten gentlemen's agreement with our sources to never report misconduct off the field.

But then came the Civil Rights Movement, the Kennedy assassination, Vietnam, and Watergate. All these huge stories of the 1960s and early '70s had a trickle-down effect. Suddenly sports writers were asking questions sports writers had never before asked, and the dynamic between sports writers and the people they covered changed dramatically.

Gone were the days when it behooved professional players or coaches to have a good relationship with reporters because good press enhanced their chances of getting the good off-season jobs that they needed to supplement their incomes.

The new breed of sports writers was called "chipmunks" because they were pesky, relentless, disruptive, and annoying. Inevitably, this strained the relationships between writers and the people they covered. Nobody trusted anybody anymore. And as salaries escalated to where college coaches were making millions, they began blowing off writers and reporters because they didn't need them anymore.

I never wanted to be an investigative reporter. It takes a lot of time and grunt work, and often there's nothing to show at the end because suspicions cannot be supported by facts. In addition, investigative reporters aren't every popular with anybody except their editors. That's the price they pay for doing the most essential jobs in journalism — being the watchdogs who expose fraud, abuse, dishonesty, and cheating. Nevertheless, stories that required investigative reporting just seemed to keep dropping into my lap.

The first was the 1968 Kentucky Derby, when a then-illegal medication was found in the post-race urinalysis of Dancer's Image, the first and only winner ever disqualified in the classic race's 144-year history.

The news broke on the Tuesday after the Derby and the newsroom at the *C-J* was in chaos when I got there around 4 p.m. As the night wore on, a lot of Derby stories came over the Associated Press wire. In one of them, Peter Fuller, the owner of Dancer's Image, claimed that somebody had "gotten" to his horse, giving him the illegal medication while he was in his stall in Barn 24 at Churchill Downs.

"Is Dancer's Image still here?" I asked my friend Jim Bolus.

Assured that he was, I suggested to Jim that we go by Barn 24 after work just to check out security. On the way to the track, we stopped by a White Castle to pick up a sack of sliders. From there we went directly to the track.

Parking outside the stall of Dancer's Image, we made no effort to be secretive. I even wadded up the empty bag from White Castle as loudly as I could. But nothing moved inside Barn 24. Looking into the barn's small office, we found the security guard fast asleep. We could easily have slipped into the Dancer's stall and given him anything.

The *C-J* ran our story on Page One, and the AP put it on the national wire. A few days later, at the request of managing editor George Gill, I returned to Barn 24 to take some photos so the editors could see the barn's layout.

As I was leaving, I heard a voice shout, "Hey, you!" I looked up to see Dr. Alex Harthill, who had been the veterinarian for Dancer's Image during his Louisville stay and who had been identified by *Sports Illustrated* as the prime suspect because of a long rap sheet of illegal activity. Playing dumb, I stuck out my hand, smiled, and said, "You must be Dr. Harthill."

Next think I knew, I was lying flat on my back with Harthill standing over me, screaming something about me investigating a gambling coup regarding the Derby future book run by the track in Caliente, Mexico. He had sucker-punched me and looked angry enough to do more if we didn't get out of there in a hurry, which I did after retrieving my glasses from where Harthill had knocked them.

I've never understood why the *C-J* didn't file charges against Harthill or even run a story about the attack. But word reached *Sports Illustrated* in New York very quickly, and it led managing editor Andre Laguerre, who loved horse racing, to offer me a job. My first day in the office, senior editor Jerry Tax told me, "If anybody ever hits you while you're working for us, we'll have the New York attorney general on his doorstep within an hour."

At *SI* from 1968–72, I largely avoided controversy, with one exception. In late January 1972, I was assigned to cover the Ohio State-Minnesota basketball game. The winner would become the front-runner in the Big Ten. It was my first game in Williams Arena, a drafty barn of a place where the Gophers still play, and I was impressed by how excited the S.R.O. crowd was.

Minnesota's rookie coach, Bill Musselman, was an intense, steely-eyed man whose motto was "Defeat is worse than death because you have to live with defeat." He had gotten into the heads of his players, who took the floor understanding that defeat was not an option. Nevertheless, with forty-four seconds to play, the Buckeyes had an insurmountable eight-point lead in those days before the three-point shot.

When seven-foot Ohio State center Luke Witte went up for an easy layup, he was fouled hard by Minnesota's Clyde Turner and knocked to the floor. Extending a hand to help Witte to his feet in an apparent act of sportsmanship, Minnesota's Corky Taylor kneed Witte in the groin when he was about halfway up, sending him back to the floor and touching off the most frightening riot I've ever seen.

Minnesota's players, most notably future baseball Hall-of-Famer Dave Winfield, punched the Ohio State players while fans streamed out of the stands to join the melee. No security was in sight because the police were outside, preparing to direct traffic. It took them a couple of minutes to reach the floor, a scary time in which someone could have been hurt badly, even killed. The remaining seconds of the game were not played.

Early the next morning, I found myself on the same plane that was taking the Buckeyes to Columbus. Noticing Witte's bandaged, bruised, and battered face, I interviewed him and other players during the flight. This enabled me to write a powerful piece that blasted Musselman for creating the atmosphere that led to the riot.

The editors loved my story and tried to talk Andre Laguerre into taking Walt Frazier of the New York Knicks off the cover and replacing it with my story. He decided to stick with Frazier but later admitted he had made a mistake. My story attracted an avalanche of letters, mostly from Minnesota, and earned me an invitation to be on the *Today* show. Unfortunately, I got pushed aside by a fresher story, but, hey, that's show biz. The outcome was that the Big Ten penalized Minnesota but not harshly enough, in my opinion.

By the time I returned to Louisville in 1972, the Dancer's Image case still was in the legal system. The courts eventually upheld the track stewards' original ruling, disqualified Dancer's Image to last, and awarded the trophy to second-place Forward Pass of Calumet Farm. I think that was baloney. For the record, I believe that Dancer's Image was, is, and always will be the winner of the 1968 Kentucky Derby.

I didn't return to the *C-J* as a sports writer because I wanted to see if I could succeed in doing another kind of reporting and writing.

Because WHAS television had just done a special series on Louisville being an "open city" in regard to illegal gambling, my first assignment was to look for new material on that. For a couple of months, George Gill and I met secretly in Central Park every two weeks, so he could give me a paycheck, and I could update him on my progress. I wasn't making much headway until I met a bookmaker who told me that a month before the Derby two races would be fixed on the Derby Day card. He said a horse named Scotch Thorn would win the seventh and another named Postal Milagro would win the race after the Derby.

Much to my astonishment, that's exactly what happened. A jockey named Jimmy Combest was brought in from Detroit to ride both horses. And the veterinarian for both was — you guessed it — Dr. Alex Harthill. At that point, we brought in Bolus, who knew a lot more about Churchill and the cast of characters than I did.

Our series ran in the summer of 1972 and led Bill May, the chairman of the Kentucky State Racing Commission, to implement some new policies, including the hiring of the respected Keene Daingerfield to be the state's chief steward. The *C-J* entered our series in a number of contests, and much to our surprise, we won the prestigious Sigma Delta Chi award for general reporting and the National Headliners Club award for investigative reporting.

As fate would have it, the Sigma Delta Chi award presentation was to be made on Derby Day, 1973, in Omaha, Nebraska. Neither Bolus nor I wanted to go because the Derby favorite that year was a colt named Secretariat. But George Gill insisted that one of us had to go to Omaha to accept the award because, after all, the runners-up in our category were a couple of young *Washington Post* reporters named Bernstein and Woodward who were working on a story called Watergate.

And so it came to be that while Jim was watching Secretariat win the first leg of his Triple Crown tour de force, I was in Omaha, sharing a stage with Carl Bernstein. He and Woodward had won a Sigma Delta Chi award for investigative reporting (we were second).

That ended my investigative reporting career until 1985. By then I was the *C-J* sports editor, and I received calls from two breeders in Central Kentucky who told me UK Basketball coach Joe B. Hall was scalping tickets in exchange for breeding rights to certain stallions. I didn't want to give up my sports column to go back into investigative reporting, so I turned the information over to David Hawpe, then the *C-J*'s managing editor, who in turn assigned Rich Whitt, who had won a Pulitzer for his coverage of the 1977 Beverly Hills Supper Club tragedy, to check it out.

Whitt couldn't confirm anything for the record — I told you investigative reporting could be frustrating — but the *Lexington Herald-Leader*, then under the inspired leadership of John Carroll, heard what Whitt was doing and launched its own investigation of UK basketball. Like Whitt, the *Herald-Leader* reporters assigned to the story couldn't prove that Hall was scalping tickets, but they turned their investigation into a new direction when several current and former players told them about receiving payments from boosters —"Fifty-dollar handshakes," they were called — after good performances.

The day that story broke, Hawpe came into my office and said, "You don't think they can win a Pulitzer, do you?" I told him I thought they had a shot, and sure enough, the *H-L* won the 1985 Pulitzer for investigative reporting, which certified it as a serious challenger to the *C-J*'s long-standing dominance in the Commonwealth.

Only a few years later, while the UK fan base still was seething over the *Herald-Leader* investigation, an Emery Air Freight envelope broke open on a conveyor belt in Los Angeles and out spilled $1,000 in cash. The envelope was addressed to Claud Mills, father of UK recruit Chris Mills, and the return address was the UK basketball office.

And so began another investigation.

Although nobody ever admitted to putting the money in the envelope, a scandal developed on another front when it was learned that somebody had taken UK player Eric Manuel's college entrance exam for him. My main role in this one was getting the first one-on-one interview with Wildcat Coach Eddie Sutton, who denied knowing about any wrongdoing. I wanted to believe him because I liked Eddie as both a person and a coach, but UK President David Roselle, a stickler for doing things right, fired both Sutton and Athletics Director Cliff Hagan.

He replaced Hagan with C.M. Newton, who somehow talked a young coach named Rick Pitino into leaving the New York Knicks to undertake the massive rebuilding job at UK. Pitino did an extraordinary job in his eight years, taking the Wildcats to three Final Fours and winning the 1996 NCAA championship.

After leaving UK after the 1997 season, Pitino spent 3 1/2 years trying to restore the Boston Celtics to the glory days under coaches Red Auerbach and Bill Russell. It didn't work out for him, even though he also was in charge of basketball operations, so he resigned in 2001 and waited for the offers to come rolling in. His former worshippers at UK didn't mind that he returned to college basketball, but they were outraged that he would take the job of replacing Denny Crum at hated rival Louisville.

I'll discuss elsewhere how that came out.

Chapter Seven

GENIUSES I HAVE KNOWN

At some point in your life, if you are lucky, you'll be able to work for or with somebody who is so bright, so good at what they do, that they approach genius. If that ever happens, pay attention. Watch them and learn. You may never approach their level, but you still will pick up some things that make you better.

I put Andre Laguerre in that level. He hired me to join the staff at *Sports Illustrated* in 1968, and I quickly learned he was regarded with reverence on the 20th floor of the Time-Life Building, where *SI* had its editorial offices in those days.

He was a graying, rumpled bear of a man who loved cigars and Scotch. A native of France, his background was in news, not sports, although he dearly loved horse racing of all kinds. I wanted to ask him about being an aide to Gen. Charles de Gaulle during World War II but never worked up the nerve.

When Time Inc. founder Henry Luce picked him as *SI*'s managing editor in 1960, the magazine, which had been launched in 1954, was drowning in red ink.

One of the first things Andre did was change the magazine's personality. In its struggling early years, it was aimed at the leisure class. So, it had a lot of stuff about subjects — bridge, yachting, polo, etc. — that were completely foreign to the middle-class sports fan who liked the magazine's pieces on college sports, baseball, and horse racing.

Then he went out and hired the best sports writers and editors he could find. From Miami, he got John Underwood. From Fort Worth, Dan Jenkins. From Salt Lake City, Bob Ottum. Each had different styles and egos, but LaGuerre was nothing if not a writer's editor. He paid far better salaries than newspapers were paying at the time, and he supplemented that with expense accounts that were incredibly generous. One of the *SI* legends was that Jenkins once got $27,000 behind on his expense accounts, and LaGuerre just let it go.

He also put together a team of brilliant photographers. Before anyone, he recognized the talent in a chubby little red-headed kid named Neil Leifer. He found another young guy with Hollywood good looks, name of Walter Iooss, who inevitably became the lead photographer on the swimsuit issue. Jerry Cooke became a fixture at the major horse races, Herbie Scharfman at championship fights. And there were so many others who were just as good — Heinz Kleutmeier, Jim Drake, John Hanlon, and several others.

Until 1970, *SI* was unable to publish color photos on late-breaking news stories. But Andre brought "fast color" to the magazine. In other words, the magazine gained the capacity to be on newsstands on Wednesday with color photos shot as late as the previous Monday. This was considered a major break-through in magazine journalism.

I played a very minor role in the historic switch to "fast color." Andre decided its first major test would be the first Ali-Frazier fight on Monday night, March 8, in Madison Square Garden, only a few blocks away from the *SI* offices. The fight was scheduled to be on the magazine's cover. However, if there was a glitch in the process, Andre had a backup cover story ready to go — my piece making the case that Indiana's swimming team might be the greatest college team ever assembled in any sport.

Although the fight pictures were a bit dark, the system worked. The fight made the cover, and my Indiana swimming story ran a week or two later. But "fast color" took *SI* to a new level, and pretty soon, black-and-white photos appeared in the magazine only rarely.

After LaGuerre left *SI* in 1974, he began a new publication called *Classic*, which was devoted exclusively to horses of all kinds. I was flattered that he asked me to do a couple of pieces for his new venture. The magazine was never intended to have a large circulation; it was merely a matter of LaGuerre indulging his passion as the final act of a historic career.

It was because of Andre that I met another man whom I put in the genius category. In 1970, David "Sonny" Werblin had a colt named Silent Screen that was one of the favorites for the Kentucky Derby. Andre assigned me to follow Werblin and his entourage through Derby week and do a sidebar on them, win or lose.

Born in the Flatbush section of Brooklyn in 1910, Werblin attended Rutgers University, and after a brief stint as a copy boy at the *New York*

Times, he joined the Music Corporation of America in 1932. At the time, MCA was the nation's leading talent agency, placing its clients in movies and Broadway plays. He was on the fast track to eventually being known as "Mr. Show Business." In 1938, he married Leah Ray Hubbard, a lead singer with the Phil Harris Orchestra, and they remained married until his death in 1991.

Although he had represented such clients as Elizabeth Taylor and Bob Hope in the 1940s, Werblin's career went to a new level with the advent of television in the late 1940s. His clients included Jackie Gleason, Milton Berle, and Johnny Carson. But in addition to representing them, he began putting together hit shows, mostly for NBC. By 1962, MCA had built such a monopoly on talent and shows that the federal government ruled it was a monopoly and ordered it to be broken up in divisions.

Werblin turned his interest from show business to sports, talking some of his buddies from Monmouth Park in New Jersey into buying the New York Titans of the fledgling American Football League. Werblin changed the team's nickname to the Jets and its colors to green-and-white in honor of St. Patrick's Day, which also was his birthday.

In 1965, Werblin shocked the sports world — and began the AFL's merger with the NFL — by paying a $427,000 bonus to Alabama quarterback Joe Namath, who had also been drafted by the NFL's St. Louis Cardinals. He had learned the power of star power in his show business days, Werblin said, and was applying it to football. It wasn't long before Namath, a bachelor playboy, was nicknamed "Broadway Joe" and appeared on an *SI* cover with Times Square in the background.

His partners became jealous that Werblin was getting all the attention, so they bought him out before the 1968 season, giving him $1.2 million for his original $250,000 investment. Unfortunately for Werblin, that was the season Namath led the Jets to the AFL title and a shocking upset of the Baltimore Colts in Super Bowl III.

But Werblin couldn't feel too badly because Silent Screen, running in the name of the Eberon Stable he owned with his wife, was named the champion 2-year-old of 1969. Trained by Bowes Bond and ridden by Johnny Rotz, he got the movie-star treatment when he got to Churchill Downs, mostly because of "Mr. Show Business."

The Werblin entourage included Toots Shor, the famed New York restauranteur, and Robert Sarnoff, who had hired a lot of Werblin's talent when he was one of the top executives at NBC and RCA. At the time, they were considerably older than yours truly, but I quickly figured out there was no way I could keep up with them in the drinking and partying departments. They began the day with Bloody Marys and ended it with brandy and cigars, or, in Werblin's case, a lethal concoction known as "Black Russians."

On Derby Day, Silent Screen had the lead in the stretch before fading to fifth. If Werblin were disappointed, he didn't show it. He just shrugged and headed back to the hotel for more drinking. He later told reporters that seeing Silent Screen finish fifth in the Derby was "the greatest experience of my life," quite a statement considering what he had seen and done.

Werblin's horses were insured by Ed McGrath, a Lloyd's of London agent based in Louisville. Through Ed and his wife Eva, I kept up with Sonny, running into him at various parties and tracks. In 1977, he told me over breakfast at Saratoga about his plans to take a swamp in New Jersey, just across the Hudson River from New York City, and turn it into a sports complex called "The Meadowlands." It would have a horse track, of course, but also a football stadium and a basketball arena.

That turned out to be Sonny's last great triumph. When the New York Giants of the NFL moved their home games to The Meadowlands, Werblin was asked what he thought about a New York team playing in New Jersey. "Pave the Hudson," he said, "and you've got 13th Avenue." In other words, The Meadowlands was a part of the Greater New York area.

In Kentucky, I met two men who were more or less Werblin disciples when it came to running race tracks — John Battaglia and William H. King. Like Werbin, both believe the customers always came first, that their tracks must be spotlessly clean, that the product must be good, and that ticket and concessions prices should never reach the gouging level.

While Battaglia ran the Latonia (now Turfway) and Miles Park (now defunct) tracks for the Emprise Corporation, William H. King was an innovator who promoted Muhammad Ali's first professional fights, made a lot of money with his Sport-Boat-Vacation shows in Louisville and Florida, and owned the Louisville Downs Harness Racing track.

Seeing the future of gambling and cable TV before just about anybody, King started an operation he called "Call-A-Bet" at Louisville Downs. The deal was that customers could deposit money with the track, place bets on the phone, and then watch the races on cable TV.

When he tried to sell Churchill Downs on the concept, track management initially laughed.

But the last laugh belonged to King, who sold his franchise to Churchill for a lot more money that he wanted earlier, so Churchill could open its own Twin Spires betting site and be a partner in the TVG live racing channel on cable TV.

William T. Young was one of the smartest business leaders ever produced in Kentucky. He was involved with a number of ventures — moving and storage, peanut butter, the soft-drink industry — and everything he touched turned to gold. He also was self-effacing and humble, preferring to stay in the background and let others take the credit.

When John Y. Brown Jr. was elected Governor of Kentucky in 1979, he staffed his cabinet with the best and brightest minds he could find, and Young was one of those who served for the grand sum of $1 per year. He became especially dear to my heart when he became chairman of the board at Transylvania and virtually saved the university with his time, talent, and treasure.

I didn't really get to know him until he plunged into the Thoroughbred business. I think it had a lot to do with his daughter Lucy, who married the French trainer Francois Boutin. It wasn't his way to go into anything halfway, so he established Overbrook Farm, hired the great D. Wayne Lukas to be his main trainer, and set out to win the grandest prizes in the sport.

He introduced Overbrook Farm to the racing world at the 1985 Breeders' Cup at Aqueduct in New York. His Storm Cat finished in a photo finish with Tasso, and Young was so confident of victory that he made his way to the winner's circle, only to sheepishly slink away when Tasso was declared the winner. "I swore then," he told me later, "that I would never again leave my seat until the results were official."

I remembered that in 1996, when Young's Grindstone was involved in a photo finish with Cannonier in the Kentucky Derby. The stewards seemed to take forever to study the finish-line photo, but Young didn't budge from his clubhouse seat. Finally, when Grindstone was declared the winner, he moved toward the infield victory stand to claim the trophy that every Kentucky horseman wants to win most of all.

Whenever I wrote something he especially liked, Young would send me a handwritten note on Overbrook stationery. But in 1998, when I wrote a column about the death of my cat Ozzie, I received a call from

Lucy Boutin. She told me that she and her father had been so touched by my piece that they would like to name one of their best Storm Cat foals after my cat.

I was flabbergasted. At the time, Storm Cat, the same horse who had lost that photo finish at Aqueduct, was the No. 1 stallion in the world. It cost a small fortune to breed a mare to him. So, now the Youngs wanted to name one of their own Storm Cat colts after my cat? This was amazing beyond belief.

I didn't think any more about it until one night in August 2001. I was driving home after a round of golf when I got a call from Mr. Young. He told me that Ozzie Cat, now a 2-year-old, was making his first start the next afternoon at Saratoga, and would I be interested in going to the races on his private plane?

At 7 a.m. the next morning, my wife Jan and I were at the private hangar at Blue Grass Field, where Mr. Young kept his plane. It was a Learjet fixed up fancy enough for a king. When I complimented Mr. Young, he, typically, waved a hand of dismissal. "It's not so much for me," he said, "but my kids and grandkids love it."

At the Saratoga airport, we were met by two black limousines that took us directly to the track, where we were ushered through the crowd to the VIP room for lunch. When it came time for Ozzie Cat's race, Mr. Young insisted that I accompany him to the paddock, where he repeatedly introduced me like this: "This is my friend Billy Reed from Kentucky, and we named this colt after his de-ceased cat."

Ozzie did himself proud. He looked like a winner in mid-stretch but tired at the end and finished second. Lukas said he liked what he saw. And then it was time to head back to the airport, albeit without Mr. Young, who was staying in Saratoga for a few days. When we were seated, Mr. Young's son and namesake asked if it was okay with us if the plane did a little detour to drop him off at Martha's Vineyard. Okay? Was he kidding? We were literally living the dream.

The next year, Lukas put Ozzie Cat on the Kentucky Derby trail, sending him to California to prep. But he just didn't have what it took and quickly ran himself out of contention. That fall, however, Mr. Young entered him in a race on Oct. 20 at Keeneland and once more invited me to join his party. This time the colt did a great impersonation of Storm Cat, his sire, and Pat Day rode him to an easy victory.

I think Mr. Young really enjoyed escorting me to the winner's circle.

Chapter Eight

I MISS CROSLEY FIELD

There's always been one cardinal rule for sports writers covering a game: No cheering in the press box. You must check your feelings at the door because a press box, or press row, is a professional workplace. No matter what he's feeling inside, a journalist is expected to be impartial when on the job.

The only sport where cheering is allowed, even encouraged, is horse racing. Tracks put betting windows in their press boxes to make it easier for the media types to gamble. When you gamble, it's only natural to root for your horse in the stretch. Writers do a better job of hiding their feelings when they win than when they lose. Once, for example, Andy Beyer of the *Washington Post* became so upset after a loss at old Gulfstream Park that he punched a hole in a press box wall. Rather than repair it, management put a frame around it so nobody could miss the "Andy Beyer Memorial Hole."

Other than horse racing, I was never guilty of cheering in the press box. But it was difficult when I was covering the Cincinnati Reds because they were, and are, the one team, college or pro, that I've followed religiously as far back as I can remember. I think I knew that Ewell "The Whip" Blackwell was the Reds' pitching ace before I knew that Harry Truman was President of the U.S.

Almost everyone in Kentucky followed the Reds for a simple geographic reason: They were the big-league team closest to where we lived. It was the same reason that baseball fans in far western Kentucky mostly pulled for the St. Louis Cardinals.

The closer you lived to a team, the clearer the radio signal from their stadiums. On hot summer nights before everybody had air conditioning, you could walk through almost any neighborhood and hear Waite Hoyt, the "voice of the Reds," or, in western Kentucky, Jack Buck or Harry Caray of the Cardinals.

The proof of my long-standing Reds' fandom is a blurry photograph of me outside the players' gate at Crosley Field, getting the autograph of a journeyman pitcher named Clarence "Bud" Podbielen. I believe it was taken in the summer of 1953, around the time I turned ten.

The Reds had a bad team that year, but they also had slugging first-baseman Ted Kluszewski, whose biceps were so big he had to cut off the sleeves of his uniform shirt, and Gus Bell, an excellent center fielder from Louisville obtained in a trade with the Pittsburgh Pirates.

To this day, my all-time favorite Reds' team isn't the fabled "Big Red Machine" of 1975 and '76. I saw those teams through the eyes of an adult, and that's not the same as following a club through the star-struck eyes of a kid, as I did with the Reds of 1956.

The Reds were very good that year, battling the Brooklyn Dodgers and Milwaukee Braves throughout the season before finally settling for third place. Their pitching was only so-so, but they had a slugging lineup that hit 221 home runs, tying the major-league record set by the New York Giants.

They wore sleeveless uniform shirts with red T-shirts underneath, and I thought that was cool. They also televised many of their home games, which meant I could watch them while staying with my grandparents in Mt. Sterling. But, mostly, they were the first Reds team to have a black star. In his rookie season, left-fielder Frank Robinson led the team with thirty-eight homers, tying the big-league record for a rookie, and established himself as a future Hall-of-Famer.

To this day, I believe that Robinson is the best all-around player in Reds' history. He hit for average and power, he ran the bases fearlessly, and his defense was more than adequate. Mostly, he was a leader both on the field and in the clubhouse. Unlike Jackie Robinson (no relation), Frank was not one to turn the other cheek when challenged. During the '56 season, he once slid into third base so hard that he got into an epic fight with Eddie Mathews of the Braves.

When the Reds traded Robinson to the Baltimore Orioles in December 1965, I got the news on the radio as I was driving to cover a basketball game at Morehead State. I swear, I was so upset that I almost drove right off U.S. 60 and into the bushes. As I recognized instantly, it was one of the worst trades in baseball history. All the Reds got in exchange were a so-so pitcher in Milt Pappas and a couple of journeymen who never helped the Reds one iota.

Although Robinson was only thirty-one at the time of the trade, Reds' general manager Bill DeWitt said he was "an old 31," which was total bull. He was so old that he won the American League's Triple Crown in 1966 (tops in batting average, homers, and runs batted in) while teaming with another Robinson, third-baseman Brooks, to lead the Orioles to a World Series victory over the Dodgers. He was voted the league's MVP, making him the first player ever to win that honor in each league.

The real reason the Reds traded Robinson was race. One night in the early 1960s, he was arrested in a Cincinnati burger joint and jailed for carrying a concealed handgun. The team's management immediately jumped to the conclusion that he might have a negative influence on Vada Pinson, the immensely talented young centerfielder who had followed Robinson at McClymonds High School in Oakland. The truth was, Pinson never would have been as good as he was — and he was plenty good — had it not been for Robinson's mentorship early in his career.

In 1970, the "Big Red Machine" was born when Johnny Bench, Tony Perez, and Pete Rose led Cincinnati to the World Series, where they were dominated by — you guessed it — Frank Robinson and the Orioles. The team got off to a slow start the next season, causing *Sports Illustrated* to send me out to do a piece on why the "Machine" had become a clunker. It was on that assignment that I got to meet both Sparky Anderson, the team's shrewd manager, and Ted Kluszewski, my boyhood hero who was then the Reds' hitting coach.

The "Big Red Machine" that won the World Series back-to-back in 1975 and '76 was a writer's dream. Besides ranking among the best teams in baseball history, they had a diverse and interesting cast of characters. The starting eight included three Hispanics (first-baseman Tony Perez, shortstop Dave Concepcion, and center-fielder Cesar Geronimo), three African Americans (second-baseman Joe Morgan, left-fielder George Foster, and right-fielder Ken Griffey Sr.), and two Caucasians (catcher Johnny Bench, who had some American Indian in his pedigree, and third-baseman Pete Rose).

I always felt the Hispanic players got cheated out of some publicity because none of the Reds' press corps could speak Spanish fluently. So, on a tough deadline after a night game, the go-to guys were Bench, Rose, and Morgan because they were both good interviews and easy to understand. If I had it to do over, I would take Spanish in high school and college instead of French because many of today's baseball players and jockeys are Hispanic.

Sparky Anderson, the manager, was extremely good with the media. I especially liked it when he would get irritated by some TV airhead and began lacing his comments with expletives so the guy would have nothing he could put on the air. He was a chess master both on the field and in the clubhouse, always anticipating and usually making the right moves.

His genius was in treating all his players fairly but not treating them alike. He gave special consideration to his superstars because they had earned it. Probably the second worst trade in Reds' history came after the 1976 season, when they sent Perez to Montreal. The "Big Doggy," as he was known, was the clubhouse catalyst who kept everything going smoothly. He knew how to deflate the egos of his fellow stars and make the others feel as if they were important.

I'm disappointed and disgusted with Rose, whom I first interviewed as a rookie in 1963 and covered until the 1989 gambling scandal that cost him his job.

We all knew that Rose was driven by ego, but Reds fans loved him just the same because he was one of them, a kid from a blue-collar background. He was not unfamiliar with the corner bar and the local bookie. Naturally, it was assumed that he loved his hometown just as much and would never leave. But when he became a free agent after the 1978 season, he was on the market quicker than you can say "Charlie Hustle."

He and his agent shopped him to the highest bidder. I got a tip that he was meeting John Galbreath, owner of the Pittsburgh Pirates, at the Campbell House in Lexington after Galbreath had given him a tour of his Darby Dan Farm.

Sure enough, there they were, eating lunch with various agents and lawyers. I didn't bother them until they were done. Naturally, both were non-committal, but knowing that Pete loved the horses almost as much as he loved baseball, I kind of thought he might wind up a Pirate.

Instead, he picked the Philadelphia Phillies, where he moved to first base because the team also had a pretty good third-baseman named Mike Schmidt. In 1981, with Morgan and Perez also on the board, Schmidt and Rose led the Phillies to victory in the World Series.

Moving to Montreal for the first part of the 1984 season, Rose returned to Cincinnati as player-manager late that year. He never officially retired as a player but just stopped putting himself in the lineup. He did a commendable job of building the team that won the 1990 World Series for Lou Piniella with a sweep over the favored Oakland Athletics.

Though Rose was barred from baseball for gambling on the Reds during his time as manager, I argued that Pete belonged in the Hall of Fame strictly because of what he had done as a player. I forgave him even after he went to prison for failing to pay taxes on memorabilia sales.

But late in the fall of 2017, after the Reds had put up a statue of Rose outside of Great American Ball Park, Rose admitted to having a sexual relationship in the early 1970s with a fourteen-year-old girl when he was a thirty-two-year-old with a wife and two kids. His only excuse was that he thought the girl was sixteen. That did it for me. I immediately wrote that if the Reds had any sense of decency, they would remove the statue and take down the banner inside the park with Rose's No. 14 on it.

Some things, my friends, are far more important than sport

Between 1976 and the present, the Reds have been to the World Series only once, shocking the Oakland Athletics with that four-game sweep in 1990. But the stars of that team — Barry Larkin, Jose Rijo, Eric Davis, etc. — never captivated the public like the stars of the "Big Red Machine." As a result, the Reds have become a franchise living in the past. Go to Great American Ball Park on any given day, and you're likely to see as many jerseys with "Rose" or "Bench" on the back as the team's current stars.

Naturally, I was thrilled when the Reds shifted their Class AAA affiliation from Indianapolis to Louisville, where the Redbirds had become the Bats. From around 2007 to 2014, the Reds had a strong farm system that produced talents such as Joey Votto, Jay Bruce, Aroldis Chapman, Todd Frazier, Billy Hamilton, and others. It was a treat for me to see them here before I saw them in Cincinnati.

I need to tell you a story on myself.

In 1962, I was covering a Reds game in which pitcher Joey Jay got knocked out early. I was accustomed to covering high school sports, where you got as near the action as you could. I know everybody wanted to know what Jay thought, but when I looked around the press box at Crosley Field, nobody was heading for the clubhouse.

Thinking I would scoop them all, I left my seat, took the rickety old elevator to the ground floor, and walked into the Reds' clubhouse. There, sitting on a stool before his locker, was Jay, head down and a beer in one hand. He was a study in dejection.

Undeterred, I walked up to him and said, "Mr. Jay, I'm Billy Reed from the *Lexington Leader* and I'd like to ask you a couple of questions."

At first he didn't move. And then he slowly raised his head to where he could regard me with bleary eyes.

"The...*Lexington*...*Leader*," he said. "Aw, f---."

And then he dropped his head again, which was my clue that the interview was over. I hustled out of there and back up to the press box, where I was relieved to see that nobody had noticed that I was gone.

Chapter Nine

RED ROSES, MINT JULEPS, AND THAT SONG

Every morning when I was in the seventh grade at DuPont Manual in Louisville, my school bus would go past Churchill Downs. On foggy winter mornings, I remember it materializing out of the mist like some great ocean liner. I never imagined that someday it would more or less be the center of my sports-writing universe.

Most of America's major sporting events — World Series, Super Bowl, Final Four, etc. — do not have a permanent home. The list of exceptions is led by the Triple Crown races, the Masters golf tournament, and the College Baseball World Series. So, how lucky was I to have my favorite sporting event located permanently in the city where I spent most of my life?

I suppose my feelings about the Kentucky Derby would qualify me as a "homer," but it's more than that. I like to think that even if I were a writer from anywhere in the world, the Derby and I would have found each other. The reason? The Derby is a writer's event, one that never fails to produce a story — or two or three — that anybody worth his or her weight in press box hot dogs can write better than he or she has ever written.

Unlike the traditional ball sports, the Derby is an acquired taste. To fully enjoy the experience, a journalist must plunge into the event's history and traditions. How did red roses, mint juleps, outlandish fashion statements, and the singing of a haunting plantation song, Stephen Collins Foster's "My Old Kentucky Home," all get wrapped up with a two-minute Thoroughbred race?

A novice to the event must learn the sport's arcane language to the point where he or she is fluent in Derby. It's important to know something about the bloodlines of both the horses and the people who care for them. It's important to know how to read the *Daily Racing Form*. For many, the task is so daunting that they only scratch the surface. They have my deepest sympathy.

My first Derby came in 1966, only a few months before I graduated from Transylvania. I had learned about the sport from Joe Hirsch at Keeneland and written enough stories about it that I felt comfortable enough to tackle the Derby.

That year the first Saturday in May at Churchill Downs was blessed by warm and breezy sunshine, and I soaked in as much of the action as possible. It was the last year of the old press box, and one of the first people I saw when I walked in was Joe Namath, the playboy quarterback from Alabama who had shocked the football world a couple of years earlier by spurning the NFL to take a $427,000 bonus — incredible money then — to play for the upstart American Football League's New York Jets.

It was explained to me that Namath was there as a guest of Joe Hirsch, with whom he shared an apartment in New York City. That gave me the entrée I needed to interrupt Namath's study of the *Daily Racing Form* to introduce myself and get a quick interview about football. I remember that he was wearing a blue jacket made of some shiny material that made him stand out in the press box like a neon sign.

I loved all of it except the infield. Although it wasn't nearly as crowded then as it is now, it still was mainly a place for college kids to get drunk and crazy. Most of them didn't care if they ever saw a horse in the flesh. But I did. I wanted to be up there in the press box, typing a Derby story in the company of the greatest sports writers in the nation.

The winner that year was Kauai King, owned by Mike Ford, an Omaha businessman; trained by Henry Forrest, a veteran of the Kentucky racing circuit; and ridden by Don Brumfield of Nicholasville, always a leading jockey at both Churchill and Keeneland. I was there in the cramped jockeys' room, sweating and jostling with others to get close to Brumfield, when he uttered the line for which Derby historians always will remember him: "I'm the happiest hillbilly hardboot in the world."

I was so charmed by it all that I promised myself I'd never miss another Derby if I could help it, and I've kept that promise with two exceptions. In another chapter, you can read why I missed Secretariat's record-shattering performance in 1973. My other absence came in 1994, when my older daughter Amy graduated from Duke University. So, when Go for Gin came splashing home on a muddy track at Churchill Downs, I was in Amy's apartment, watching with her and other family members. And you know what? I was exactly where I should have been.

Earlier, I mentioned the old press box at Churchill. It was replaced in 1967 by the biggest and best press box in the country. High atop the clubhouse, it afforded an unobstructed view of the entire track, enabling the media to see every step through binoculars if they wished. But what made it different from the old press box was its size. It was big enough to give the biggest names in American sports journalism — Red Smith of New York, Jim Murray of Los Angeles, Blackie Sherrod of Dallas, etc. — both a seat on the deck outside overlooking the track and working space inside.

Now Churchill Downs is about the only major sporting venue in North America that doesn't have a press box. During one of the track's late 1990s renovations, management decided to demolish the best press box in the sport and replace it with a smaller version. When that dastardly deed was done, management checked out the magnificent view and decided to turn it into very expensive club known as "The Mansion." The press was downgraded to a windowless room under the grandstand and near the paddock. It was a sad bit of irony, considering that the Derby became what it is today largely due to the media.

When Col. Matt Winn took over Churchill Downs in 1903, the Derby was mainly a regional event that had a difficult time getting the interest of the major stables in the East. So, Winn, a promoter way ahead of his time, determined that the way to get the Eastern stables was to get the big-name writers from New York. So, he began spending his winters in an apartment at the Waldorf-Astoria, where he got to know the likes of Grantland Rice and Damon Runyan personally. He picked up so many dinner checks and bar tabs that the writers almost felt obligated to come to the Derby (at Winn's expense, of course).

As I said earlier, the Derby always produces a good story, and that was as true in the early years of the 20th century as it is now. In 1913, the winner Donerail, ridden by Roscoe Goose, paid $113 for a $2 wager. In 1915, Regret became the first female winner. In 1918, the popular Exterminator won the day at Churchill Downs. And in 1919, Sir Barton became the first Triple Crown winner, although that term wasn't coined until Charlie Hatton of the *Daily Racing Form* first used it in the 1930s.

The nationally syndicated columnists wrote the hell out of these stories, putting the Derby in position to become one of the first major

A very young Billy Reed.

Billy and his mother, Doris, Mt. Sterling, Kentucky.

Billy and his Grandad, Clell Cockrell, Mt. Sterling, Kentucky.

A young Billy in his best quarterback pose, 1953.

Outside Churchill Downs, ca. 1953.

Billy with his little sister, Judy, outside Churchill Downs in 1954.

Team photo for the Louisville Colonels baseball team, 1953.

1955 Giants, Beechnut Pony League. Billy is on the first row, third from left. Mitch McConnell not present.

The 1956 Cincinnati Redlegs.

Billy and Gordy Coleman, 1st baseman on the Cincinnati Reds' 1961 World Series team.

Joe Namath at the 1966 Kentucky Derby. Photo by Billy Reed.

Stationed at Ft. Ord, California, 1967.

With Dr. Fager in 1968, (first Sports Illustrated *story).*

With Johnny Nerud, trainer, in 1968 at Belmont Park.

With Don Schellander of Yale University, swimming star of the 1964 Olympics.

With Seth Hancock at Claiborne Farm of Paris, Kentucky in 1974.

Edward Baptista, owner of Canonero II, 1971 Preakness.

Billy with Secretariat, January 1974.

Billy (center) with Eddie Pope of the Miami Herald *and Howard Cosell at the Preakness.*

Trainer LeRoy Jolley, actor Jack Klugman, and Billy, 1980.

Dan Farley, Billy, and Joe Hirsch at Pimlico Race Course, Baltimore, Maryland.

1988 Eclipse Awards with members of Churchill Downs, pictured l-r: Karl Schmitt, Tom Meeker (President), John Asher, Jennie Rees, Billy Reed, Ben Van Hook, and Gerry Lawence.

Billy accepting the Eclipse Award in 1989, for a column he did about trainer D. Wayne Lukas winning his first Derby with the filly Winning Colors.

April 28, 1981

Billy Reed

Billy,

I was delighted to hear of the Engelhard Award which you will be presented tonight. Unfortunately, Edie and I will not be able to attend the banquet. I didn't want you to take our absence as indicating a lack of enthusiasm. I am delighted that you are being recognized for your excellent writing about the thoroughbred industry...but one of the many areas of sport with which you grace The Courier-Journal with your magnificent prose.

B.B., Jr.

Letter of congratulations from Barry Bingham Jr., Publisher of The Courier-Journal, *April 28, 1981.*

Billy poses with Dr. Fager before the 1968 Brooklyn Handicap. Note: this marks the first story Billy did for Sports Illustrated.

Mike Barry and Derby-winning trainer, Nick Zito, 1991.

Jim Bolus, Chick Lang of Pimlico Race Course, and Billy.

With William H. King of Louisville Downs.

Billy receiving an award from William Kelly of Transylvania University. Looking up is William T. Young, famous businessman and owner of Overbrook Farm.

Billy with Groom/Exercise Rider Charlie Rose, and Calumet Farm's Alydar before the Kentucky Derby, 1978.

Peter Fuller, Owner of "Dancer's Image," 1968.

Lou Cavalaris, Trainer of "Dancer's Image," 1968.

Triple Crown Winner Affirmed and trainer Laz Barrera, Kentucky Derby, 1978.

Alydar with (from right): Admiral Gene Markey, Melinda Bena, Mrs. Markey, Joseph Bena (in back), and Robert McGoodwin. Billy is in the background, left. Taken before the 1978 Blue Grass Stakes.

Actor Jack Klugman of "The Odd Couple" and "Quincy M.D." prior to the 1980 Kentucky Derby.

Pictured l-r: Mike Barry; Paul McDonald, lobbyist for Churchill Downs; Billy Reed, Courier-Journal Sports Editor; and Edgar Allen, PR director at Churchill Downs. Photo by John Nation.

AMC's Jim McKay and Mona Woods, presenting Billy with the David A. Woods Award at The Preakness Stakes, 1982.

Winning photo for "Ozzie Cat," Maiden Special Weight–$50,000, October 20, 2002.

Billy entering the locker room at the Notre Dame Stadium.

Billy at the dais during the celebrity roast of Coach Joe B. Hall.

Dean Eagle, former Courier-Journal *and* Louisville Times *Sports Editor, with Billy and basketball great Bill Walton, 1974.*

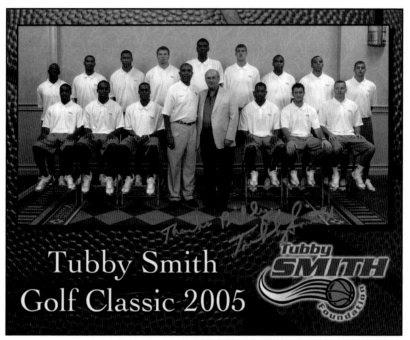

Tubby Smith and the 2005 University of Kentucky Wildcats.

Elvin "Big E" Hayes of Houston (right) arrives at Standford Field for the 1967 Final Four. With him is his teammate Don Chaney.

Billy with basketball legend Al McGuire, who coached Marquette University from 1964-77 and later worked as a college basketball television commentator for NBC.

UCLA's Lew Alcindor at Freedom Hall before the 1967 Final Four.

Billy with Denny Crum in the Univeristy of Louisville locker room at Freedom Hall.

Billy interviewing Allen Murphy, member of U of L's 1975 Final Four team.

Billy with Muhammad Ali at Deer Lake.

Muhammad Ali at his training camp in Deer Lake, Pennsylvania, before the 1978 Leon Spinks rematch. His then-wife, Veronica, came out to join them.

sporting events to be broadcast nationally on the radio (in 1925). By the time Gallant Fox became the sport's second Triple Crown leader in 1930, Col. Winn had achieved his goal of making the Derby one of the country's premier sporting events.

Today it's largely forgotten that when National Industries (owned by Stanley Yarmuth, father of Congressman John Yarmuth) attempted a hostile takeover of Churchill in 1969, the wealthy horsemen on the track's board of directors banded together to thwart it. At the time, John Galbreath, the owner of Darby Dan Farm and the track's chairman of the board, vowed that Churchill always would be owned and run by horsemen, not a corporation.But that promise became inoperable and so did the media as I had always known and loved it. Once the corporate suits gained control of Churchill, they decided the Derby no longer needed the media, especially the print variety. The track gets all the publicity it needs through its TV deals and social media. Much as I'm loath to admit it, they have a point. Still, it's impossible to imagine the World Series or Super Bowl ever being played in a stadium that has no press box.

In fairness, I also must acknowledge that I rarely watched the Derby from the press box. Many times I'd spend the day hanging around an owner or trainer if I felt they had a great shot to win. That's what happened in 1980, when I watched the Derby with actor Jack Klugman, who was best known for playing Oscar in the TV version of *The Odd Couple* and, later, for playing the lead character in *Quincy, P.I.*

I met Jack after the colt named for him, Jaklin Klugman, earned his Derby ticket by winning the Hollywood Derby. In real life, he was more or less Oscar, the sloppy sports writer of *The Odd Couple*, so we hit it off and made plans to get together when he arrived in Louisville.

One morning Derby week, Jack asked me if I could take him to Central Kentucky to see Secretariat, Seattle Slew, and Affirmed. I was able to arrange it with a couple of calls, so here we came to visit the Triple Crown winners. Jack had a purpose for this, but I didn't figure it out until he asked me to drive him directly to Jaklin's barn at Churchill. When the colt was brought out, Jack closed his eyes and began rubbing his forehead. "Here's a little Secretariat," he mumbled. "Here's a little Seattle Slew, a little Affirmed."

On Derby Day, I watched the race with Jack in his box. As the field turned for home, Jaklin Klugman was near the lead and moving well. I thought Jack had his Derby winner until his colt gave way to Genuine

Risk and Rumbo. Still, as Jack later pointed out, finishing third in the Kentucky Derby was not chopped liver.

Eight years later, I watched the Derby with mega-trainer D. Wayne Lukas in the track superintendent's little office off the tunnel leading to the track. When his big roan filly Winning Colors held off Forty Niner's late charge to become the third filly to when the Derby, it gave Lukas the victory he wanted most. Spinning, he whacked me on the arm with his rolled-up program and said, "My turn . . . my turn!" Then he bolted from the room and headed for the track to congratulate jockey Gary Stevens.

The column I did about that won me my second Eclipse Award for newspaper writing, proving there's nothing quite like being at the right place at the right time.

One reason I became so interested in the Derby was my friend Jim Bolus. I had enormous respect for Jim, and I figured that if he cared so much about something, it must be exceedingly worthwhile. We were always together on the backstretch before Derby week and, along with Mike Barry, became known as the "Three Musketeers." At least, that's what we liked to call ourselves.

I can't tell you for sure that Jim and I invented the "walk over," now a Derby tradition in which small armies of writers, photographers, and hangers-on follow a certain horse from the backstretch barn area to the tunnel leading to the paddock. However, I will tell you that when Jim and I first did it in 1968 — we followed Dancer's Image — we didn't have any company. We did it because we wanted to be close to the action instead of watching from high up in the press box.

The period from 1968 through 1980 always will be my "golden era" of horse racing. During those twelve years, we had three Triple Crown winners (Secretariat, Seattle Slew, and Affirmed), one great horse who should have been a Triple Crown winner (Spectacular Bid), the first and only disqualified winner (Dancer's Image), the second filly winner (Genuine Risk), a longshot winner from Venezuela (Canonero II), a huge upset (Bold Forbes over Honest Pleasure in 1976), a sitting U.S. President attending the Derby (Richard Nixon in 1969), and Princess Margaret of the British royal family attending the 100th Derby (won by Cannonade in 1974).

I'm pretty sure the sport never again will have an era so exciting and so full of fascinating stories.

Every Derby seems to produce a main character who puts his or her stamp on the race. In 1990, that turned out to be Carl Nafzger, a former rodeo cowboy who trained Unbridled for Mrs. Frances Genter, a longtime owner who was ninety when the Derby field went to the post. Before the race, Nafzger had agreed to wear a microphone for ABC, so the nation got to hear him call the race for Mrs. Genter in his Texas twang.

"He's taking the lead, Miz Genter. . . . You're going to win the Kentucky Derby, Miz Genter. . . . Oh, I love you, Miz Genter."

Carl and I became friends, and I talked *Sports Illustrated* into letting me do a story about him. That was a minor coup for me and editor Demmie Stathopolous because the magazine didn't devote nearly as much space to horse racing as it did when Andre Laguerre was in charge. As part of my research, I went to Florida to interview Carl and go deep-sea fishing with him. Unfortunately, it was cold and windy that day, and our boat rocked and rolled so fiercely that fishing was impossible. I spent most of the time below deck, praying and drinking a strong libation.

When the story was published, I called Carl and said, "I have good news and bad news. The good news is that the story is in the magazine and looks pretty good. The bad news is that it's in the swimsuit issue, and nobody will ever read it."

We laughed about that for years.

Chapter Ten

THE WOMEN'S MOVEMENT AND ME

I never worked with or for a woman until I joined *Sports Illustrated* in 1968. The staff in New York had several female reporters who were mainly fact-checkers looking for a chance to write. But the senior editors included Jule Campbell, who was in charge of the Swimsuit Issue; Virginia Kraft, who specialized in travel and outdoors pieces, and Patricia Ryan, who had established herself as a fine writer before moving to the editing side.

Pat was so sharp that she eventually became the editor of *People Magazine*. She had a relationship with Ray Cave, another *SI* editor who left to join *Time*, where he became the editor. Talk about a New York power couple. To have the editors of *People* and *Time* living under the same roof was fascinating material for the tabloids and media reporters. Imagine, if you can, the conversations over breakfast.

I left *SI* in 1972, the same year Congress passed Title IX into law. It mandated that all public schools that received federal money must sponsor women's athletic teams that were equal to the men's teams. Most athletics directors didn't like the new law because women's sports didn't produce revenue. Besides, since there was no sport for women equal to football for men, the schools faced the complicated challenge of balancing spending to meet the Title IX guidelines.

Back at the *C-J*, women also were starting to have more influence in the news room. Under the leadership of publisher Barry Bingham Jr., all the Bingham media properties — the *C-J*, *Louisville Times*, and WHAS radio-TV — were making serious efforts toward providing opportunities for woman and African Americans. But the woman who really stuck out was Carol Sutton, who had left reporting to run what was always known as "the women's section." Under Carol, that name was abolished because it defined the section too narrowly and replaced by the "lifestyle section."

Carol was as much addicted to good writing as she was cigarettes (she died from lung cancer in 1985). She loved long lunches that were laced with good whiskey and conversation, and she had an insatiable curiosity about the world near and far. On vacations, she liked to go to South America or Mexico.

Although she didn't care much about sports, she liked me, and I certainly liked her. I was overjoyed, in fact, when the Binghams named her to replace George Gill, making her the first female managing editor of a major American newspaper. She even got her photo on the cover of *Time*, along with other women who were breaking barriers. I told the magazine she was the best editor I'd had at the *C-J*, and my old boss, George Gill, made it clear that he didn't much like that.

One of Carol's first major decisions was replacing the popular state columnist Joe Creason, a tennis buff who had died of a sudden heart attack. I knew I would be one of the candidates, but I seriously doubted Carol would pick me, at age thirty-one, when she had more experienced talents at her disposal. But doggone if she didn't have the guts to do it. Several people at Sixth and Broadway predicted I wouldn't last, but I did the job for three-and-a-half years before applying for the sports editor's job when Dave Kindred left for the *Washington Post* in 1977.

I was determined to reward Carol for her faith in me, and I think I did. I criss-crossed the state, looking for offbeat characters and untold stories. I judged the "Miss Watermelon Bust" contest for a fraternity at Murray State, located a moonshiner near Pikeville, and covered Loretta Lynn's return to her home in Butcher Hollow — or "Holler" — as it's pronounced in Eastern Kentucky.

I also wrote about sports and athletes that the overworked sports staff couldn't get around to covering, and many of them involved women. I went to McDowell to write about female scoring sensation Geri Grigsby and to Richmond to cover the revival of the Girl's State Basketball Tournament. Obviously, due to Title IX, young women would no longer be restricted to cheerleading or intramural sports.

I like to think Jennie Rees was one way I thanked Carol Sutton.

Sometime after the 1979 or '80 Derby, Jim Bolus gave up the racing beat at the *C-J* to join the *Louisville Times*. I think he wanted to have his nights free to spend more time with his wife, Suzanne, and kids, Jim Jr. ("Bo") and Jennifer. At first Stan Slusher, our administrator, and

I agreed to give Richard Sowers a chance. But he left after a year or so, and we were back to square one.

We had a young copy editor named Jennie Rees who wanted to take a crack at the job. I met with her one day in the Churchill Downs press box, and she told me she had an offer to join the *Sporting News* in St. Louis. I didn't want to lose Jennie because she was bright, enthusiastic, and hard-working. So, I told Slusher we should give her a chance on the racing beat, and he agreed.

Well, I've never seen anybody take to a sport the way Jennie took to horse racing. The backstretch became her second home, and the trainers and jockeys loved her upbeat personality. What she lacked in height, Jennie more than made up for in heart. Slusher and I both were very pleased.

But one day, one of our bosses came into the sports department and announced, in front of the *Times* staff, that he thought the *C_J* should put a buddy of his on the racing beat, even though the guy had twice been suspended for plagiarism. The editor said that his pal would "give us Damon Runyon stuff." To which the droll *Times* copy editor Earl Vance responded, "Yeah — verbatim."

But the editor persisted until I finally told him that if he took Jennie off the racing beat, I'd quit because it just wasn't fair. That was the only time I went to the mat like that during my nine-plus years as sports editor, and it probably made me some enemies up the chain of command, but there was no more talk about replacing Jennie.

All she did, of course, was become the best racing writer in the nation. You will notice I didn't say the best *female* racing writer. She was the best, period, and she proved it by winning all manner of awards. Even after I left the *C-J* to return to *Sports Illustrated* and the *Lexington Herald-Leader*, I followed Jennie closely and always was happy when something good happened to her.

Admittedly, I didn't write much about women during my career as a columnist, but I didn't ignore them, either. When teenager Mary T. Meagher took the swimming world by storm in 1979, setting world records in the butterfly stroke, I wrote about her and began looking forward to the 1980 Olympics in Moscow, where she figured to be one of the Games' biggest winners.

Alas, however, President Carter pulled the U.S. team out of those Olympics to protest the Russian invasion of Afghanistan. So, Mary T.

had to wait until the 1984 Games in Los Angeles, where she won both butterfly events and added two more gold medals on relay teams. Every time she stood atop the awards stand and the "Star-Spangled Banner" was played, I got weepy. It was just so special to see this girl from Louisville at the pinnacle of her sport.

I also wrote a lot about female jockeys because, of all the professional sports, Thoroughbred racing is the only one where women compete against men on an absolutely equal basis. So, I wrote a long piece about jockey Mary Bacon for Carol Sutton's features section of the *C-J*, and later I did a long piece for *SI* that was built around female jockeys Julie Krone and Donna Barton.

I was there in 1993 when Krone became the first female to ride a Triple Crown winner, booting home Colonial Affair in the Belmont Stakes in New York. Unfortunately, even that didn't open many doors for female riders. Most trainers were men, and they simply could not be convinced that women were strong enough to beat the best males.

The best female rider of this century, Rosie Napravnik, quit to have children. Maybe she'll come back, and maybe she won't, but someday a female jockey is going to win the Kentucky Derby. I just hope that the one who does it is as nice as Patti Cooksey, a breast cancer survivor who is remembered as the first female to ride in the Preakness Stakes, and I hope Donna Barton — now Donna Brothers — is there to do one of her horseback interviews for NBC as the winner heads to the winner's circle.

Today, sadly, female journalists haven't made as many strides as female athletes, at least on the local level. I see women commentators on ESPN and the networks, and I read their work in some of the national publications. But the Louisville sports media, to cite one example, still is a man's world. The city has no female sports columnists, no female radio talk show hosts, no female play-by-play announcers, and no female sports directors.

The way to cure that is for women to aspire for top management jobs. Then, like Carol Sutton many years ago, they can take chances on young people, female and male alike. I've taken my granddaughter Lucy into Paul Rogers' radio booth at the University of Louisville's Papa John's Cardinal Stadium, and she seemed to like what she saw and heard.

Who knows? Maybe someday she'll be the "Voice of the Cards."

Chapter Eleven

THE SOUNDTRACKS OF MY LIFE

For years, athletes have been wrapped up in music, but it has gotten more pronounced with the advent of smart phones and other technological wonders. Every time you see players getting off a bus before a game, they all have buds plugged into their ears, listening to their music. I wonder if some even take them out when they get into the shower.

But I can relate, to a point. Going back to the 1950s, with the advent of transistor radios, I liked to take my music with me. If playing ball and learning about sports was the essence of my childhood, then Doo-Wop and other early forms of rock-n-roll was the soundtrack. I enjoyed the "sock hops" after Henry Clay High games on Friday nights as much as I enjoyed the games themselves.

Knowing how much I enjoyed early rock music, the late George Lapides, one of the best guys I ever met in sports writing, told me once that he sometimes got to hang around with Elvis Presley when he was a young guy in Memphis.

He told about the time he and Elvis happened to be in a dentist's office at the same time, and the receptionist caught Presley's attention. He told George, essentially, to bring her to one of his parties and then get lost, which George dutifully did. I loved stories like that because, as a kid, I was every bit as mesmerized by Elvis as I was, say, Mickey Mantle.

Many years later, I called George to tell him I was coming to Memphis to cover the St. Jude Classic golf tournament for *SI*. I asked if maybe he could give me a tour of the places where the young Elvis hung out. "Well, sure," he said, "but I've got something you might like even better. How would you like to meet Sam Phillips?"

That was like asking a whiskey drinker how he would like to meet Jack Daniels. Are you kidding? The heck with the golfers. They're just athletes, albeit very accomplished ones. But Sam Phillips is the genius — and I do not use that word lightly — who founded Sun Records and first recorded Elvis, Jerry Lee Lewis, Johnny Cash, Carl Perkins, Roy Orbison, Charlie Rich, and others at his little studio on a Memphis street corner.

So, George set it up, which is how I found myself sitting on a sofa in Phillips' home, listening to the great man tell stories. His house more or less looked the same as it did on Sept. 4, 1956, when Elvis, Jerry Lee, Johnny, and Carl ran into each other and had an impromptu jam session that was recorded and released as "The Million-Dollar Quartet," which became a Broadway play and a TV series.

Phillips spoke in a low, gravelly voice that sometimes was difficult to hear. Nevertheless, I was mesmerized. I remember him telling about how the young Roy Orbison came out of Texas with his band, determined to make it big in country music. But they bombed and the band went back home, leaving Roy and his bride, Claudette, to live under Sam's roof for a while. At some point Roy recorded a song named for his wife, and it was received well enough to open the way for "Only the Lonely," Orbison's first national hit, in 1960.

Of "The Million-Dollar Quartet," the only one I ever got to interview was Jerry Lee, also known as "The Killer," a piano-playing wild man out of Louisiana whose career got sidetracked when he married his 15-year-old second cousin.

It happened one night at the Beverly Hills Supper Club in northern Kentucky, which burned to the ground in 1977, killing 130 customers. On this night, Jerry Lee was so drunk or stoned that he could barely get through a song. At one point, he flung an arm into the air wildly, and next thing I knew, one of his rings fell into my lap.

I discussed the matter with Bill Malone, my friend and partner in crime on more adventures than I can remember, and we agreed the right thing to do was go to Jerry Lee's dressing room and return the ring. Well, it would be an understatement to say he was grateful. He hugged me and shook our hands.

Then I told him that his friend Carlos Toadvine, who had opened for him several times as "Little Enis and the Fabulous Table Toppers," had died young in Lexington. That led to more hugging, accompanied by blubbering. "Aw, Killer," he said. "He was a helluva guy."

Doing the *C-J's* general column from 1974–77 gave me the opportunity to indulge my curiosity about entertainers who weren't athletes.

So, I went to the Executive Inn in Evansville and interviewed Rick Nelson, who gained fame as the younger son on the *Ozzie & Harriet* television show of the 1950s. He grew out of that role and recorded a series of hit records in the late 1950s and early '60s. When he found out I was from Louisville, he recalled playing tennis there in a national juniors tournament.

At the time I interviewed him, Rick was on tour with the Stone Canyon Band, and they had a hit going for them named "Garden Party." It was about the time Rick appeared in Madison Square Garden and got booed for doing his new stuff instead of the oldies, such as "Hello, Marylou," "Poor Little Fool," and "I Believe What You Say."

He came off as a regular guy, not an international heart-throb, and I was saddened when he died in a plane crash a few years later.

And then there was the night outside Freedom Hall where I interviewed Loretta Lynn in the bedroom of her tour bus, a huge Greyhound that had been converted into a sort of mobile home.

Although I never was a big fan of hard-core country, I liked Loretta. She was the coal miner's daughter from Butcher Hollow who had a rough time getting out of the mountains and dealing with Mooney, her boozer of a husband. In fact, while Loretta and I were talking, Mooney came to the back of the bus and banged on the bedroom door.

"Mooney, you stop that," Loretta said. "I'm talking to this reporter fella from the newspaper and you leave us alone. Go to sleep!"

And I suppose he did because he didn't bother us again. I remember how tired she look that night. She had given her all for her fans, as she always did, even staying on stage and signing autographs. I left wondering how much longer she would keep going before retiring to the life of leisure she had earned.

I was personally involved with two musical groups. When I was at Henry Clay High, I joined some of my friends in the Key Club in starting a group called "The Torques," which included basketball players Bill Brooks and Bob Johnson. I worked for a while as their business manager, which mainly meant that I got to help load and unload the equipment. They once let me sing backup on Ray Charles' "What'd I Say" but elbowed me off stage because I couldn't even moan on key.

And then there were The Monarchs of Louisville, about whom I wrote a book when they reached their 50th birthday in 2010. At one time their lead singer was Butch Kauffman, who played on St. Xavier

High's 1962 state championship team and then was a valuable sub on the great Clem Haskins-Dwight Smith teams at Western Kentucky. My main connection, though, was sax player Leon Middleton, one of the founding members and a former drum major at U of L.

I well remember the night at the Kentucky State Fair when the Monarchs were the warmup act for Frankie Valli and the Four Seasons. They were so good that Frankie was furious, figuring somebody was trying to show him up. As I recall it, he threw a fit and said he wouldn't do his second show until he had a different group playing in front of him.

I regret that I never got to interview Linda Ronstadt, who is my favorite female singer of all time, but I did get to be around Judy Collins one night at Northern Kentucky University. Her voice is pure and crystalline, never failing to do a perfect interpretation of folk songs, spirituals, and ballads.

She was having a press conference before the show, and it turned out I was the only male there. This was around 1976, when the women's movement was gathering momentum. So, before Judy could take the first question, a female reporter stood, pointed at me, and said, "I don't think he belongs here. . . . Can you ask him to leave?"

Bless her heart, Judy Collins said, "Ladies, if this gentleman cares enough about me and my music to be here, I will treat him with the same respect that I treat the rest of you. Now who has a question?" I already was one of her fans, but that night she earned a special place in my heart.

In the summer of 1976, within a five-day period, Freedom Hall played host to Elvis, Elton John, and a young band named the Eagles. I did a story about it for the *C-J* Sunday magazine. I think the Elvis concert was the time when the mother of my daughters, the former Alice Shephard of Bardstown, got a kiss on the lips from Elvis.

A music major at Transylvania, Alice wasn't nearly as crazy about pop music as I was. She liked the Beatles, mostly because they were "cute," and she was crazy about John Denver. But she wanted no part of the Rolling Stones or Elvis, even though I had access to front-row tickets through my friend A.C. Chapman, who was then in charge of booking acts into Freedom Hall.

I finally got her to an Elvis concert by making her feel guilty. I told her — rightly so, I might add — that whether she liked him or not,

Elvis was an American icon, like Sinatra before him, and she should at least broaden her horizons for one night, so she could tell our kids she saw The King in person.

I was standing at the side of the stage when Elvis reached the point in his show where he got down on one knee and moved from one side of the stage to the other, wiping the sweat off his brow with towels that he then reached down and gave to a screaming fan, along with a kiss.

Well, much to my surprise, doggone if Alice wasn't right there at the stage, elbowing other ladies out of the way, so she could get a kiss. She succeeded, too, and I don't think she has spoken a harsh word about Elvis since then.

It was a bit different with Dave Kindred's wife, Cheryl. While Dave was in New York covering the UK basketball team in the 1976 NIT, I took Cheryl with me to an Elvis concert in Cincinnati. He had picked up so much weight that he literally split the seams on his tight white pants, so naturally, I wrote a column about Fat Elvis.

I'm not going to say that Cheryl was upset with my column, but I do seem to remember that it was several weeks before she spoke to me again.

Much as I still love the music of the 1950s and '60s, I can make the argument that the Big Band music of the 1930s and '40s may be the best pop stuff ever. My fondest memory of my mother, other than when she was reading to me or taking me to a Disney movie, was when she would play her 78 rpm records and tell me about the wonders of Glenn Miller, Benny Goodman, and Tommy Dorsey.

So, you will not be surprised to learn that I can't stand hip-hop or rap, especially when it's played at ear-splitting levels before ball games. My friend Leon Middleton claims it's not music because it can't be scored. I'm not sure what that means, exactly, but it sounds right.

I also get a chuckle whenever I hear one of the songs from my era played in a TV commercial or by a college pep band during a timeout. Bruce Channel's "Hey, Baby" certainly has withstood the test of time, and the UK band's version of "Gimme Some Lovin'," by the Spencer Davis Group, never fails to get the house rocking.

One of my favorite general columns was about Cowboy Steve Taylor, who operated a one-watt radio station out of his home in Lexington. Steve loved country music, unusual for an African American, and his favorite singer (one of mine, too) was Emmylou Harris.

Every day Cowboy Steve went on the air, so to speak, and did his show professionally. It made no difference to him that you couldn't find his station once you got past the sidewalk in front of his house. To watch him at work, you would think he was in Nashville, working for one of the mega-stations.

After the column appeared, I found out that Emmylou Harris was doing a Valentine's Day performance at UK. I enlisted my high school friend Frank Harscher to help me get tickets. We picked up Steve an hour or so before the show, and on the way, he insisted that we stop by a drug store and get a box of Valentine's candy that already was on sale. He wanted to give it to Emmylou.

We worked out the introduction and the presentation, then went to our seats. After her opening number, Emmylou said, "I want to dedicate this next song to Cowboy Steve Taylor, who gave me the only Valentine I got this year." And then she did her incredible version of *Sweet Dreams*.

I don't have the words to describe the look on Steve's face.

Chapter Twelve

AMERICA LOVES ITS FOOTBALL

When I got into sports writing in 1959, most of today's major events — Kentucky Derby, World Series, Masters, etc. — already were in place. But during my time, a new extravaganza was invented that surpassed all the others until now it stands alone as the holiest day on the sports calendar. I'm talking, of course, about the Super Bowl.

It arose from the chaos that came to exist in the early 1960s, when the American Football League (AFL) challenged the established National Football League (NFL) by writing big checks to get the best college talent. The tipping point came when Sonny Werblin of the AFL's New York Jets paid Alabama quarterback Joe Willie Namath the then-amazing sum of $427,00 to play in the new league.

That, more than anything, convinced NFL Commissioner Pete Rozelle to enter into serious negotiations with the AFL for a merger. The first step in that direction was a game between the league champions. And in 1969, the year before the merger became official, Namath led the Jets to a monumental upset over the Baltimore Colts in the third edition of what was to become the Super Bowl.

Today the Super Bowl is much more than a football game. Some watch the telecast for the commercials, which cost roughly the same amount as a Third World country's budget. Others watch it for the halftime show, which showcases the country's most popular singers, dancers, and bands. And still others watch it for the gambling.

On Super Bowl Sunday, the nation's capitol moves from Washington, D.C., to Las Vegas, Nev., where the casinos and sports books will literally take action on anything and everything to do with the football game. There's an over-under bet on how long the national anthem will last, who will win the pregame coin toss, and how many times the announcers will mention a certain player's wife or girlfriend. You name it and Vegas will take it.

Although the players try to look at the Super Bowl as just another game — which it really is, when you cut through all the hype — they also know that careers can be made or ruined in the most watched sporting event this side of soccer's World Cup. You don't want to be the kicker who shanks the game-winning field goal. You don't want to be the defensive back who gets beat on the game-winning touchdown. But you do want to be that guy who wins the Most Valuable Player Award and tells the worldwide TV audience that he's going to Disney World.

I covered the Super Bowl from 1979 through '86, and I still have some of the nice luggage they gave the media. But after the first couple, to tell you the truth, I could take it or leave it. The week before the game, there was one day where the writers had access to the players. Otherwise, the NFL public-relations people devoted their time to a daily press conference and making sure the media had everything it needed in the way of dinner reservations, golf tee times, tours, etc. Nice, but also pretty sterile.

Besides, I was, am, and always will be a college football guy. I've never seen anything in pro football to match a big game day in South Bend, Tuscaloosa, Ann Arbor, Austin and various other campuses around the nation. I love all of it — the fight songs, the marching bands, the cheerleaders, the mascots, and the tradition that dates back to the first college game in 1869.

However, I also must admit that my feelings began about college football began to change after the 1961 season, when the University of Kentucky hired Charlie Bradshaw, who had played and coached under the sainted Paul "Bear" Bryant, to replace Blanton Collier, a kind and gentle man who made the mistake of not winning as much as Bryant did when he was at UK from 1946 through '53.

An ex-Marine, Bradshaw had steely blue eyes that could burn holes in you. He also had a messianic quality about him that easily captivated young recruits. Shortly after taking the UK job, he recruited halfback Rodger Bird of Corbin, quarterback Rick Norton of Louisville, tackle Sam Ball of Henderson, and receiver Rick Kestner of Belfry, who all went on to careers in the NFL.

But Bradshaw also employed some conditioning methods that were downright cruel, leaving to a mass exodus of players and bringing in *Sports Illustrated* to do a scathing piece entitled "Rage to Win." He started the 1962 season with only 30 varsity players, which led to the nickname "Thin Thirty." But with all the talented freshmen waiting to join the varsity in 1963, nobody in win-hungry Lexington made an issue of Bradshaw's methods except the UK student newspaper, where a courageous young editor named David Hawpe dared to editorially ask, "What price glory?"

One of the players to leave the team was Jim Bolus, who was to become one of my dearest friends. An All-State linebacker and center from Louisville Male, Jim loved football, especially the contact part. But like future pro linebacker Dale Lindsey (who transferred to Western Kentucky) and the others who left, he also was smart enough to know the difference between conditioning and punishment. He did the right and moral thing, certainly, but Jim never quite got over the indignity of being labeled a "quitter." Trust me, he was anything but that.

Bradshaw lasted through the 1968 season and was fired because his best record was a modest 6-4. But he left an impression on me that has lasted to this day. Because football is such a violent sport, coaches tend to think of themselves more in terms of war instead of education. They are the "generals" who lead their armor-clad warriors into battle once a week. They claim that football "builds character" unlike any other sport or extra-curricular activity, a claim I have come to doubt over the years as the amount of cheating has grown in lockstep with the cost of big-time college football.

As recently as the summer of 2018, an abuse scandal unfolded at Maryland that revived my memories of Charlie Bradshaw. Haven't some of these coaches learned anything over the years? Don't they understand how society has changed? Apparently not, because many at both the college and pro level seem determined to debunk the scientific findings about how football-related concussions can often lead former players to early dementia, depression, and even suicide.

I remember the time when a discussion with my daughter Susan led us to football. She declared in no uncertain terms that she would not allow my grandsons Shephard and Sam to play football when they grew up, even if they seemed to have an aptitude for it. I thought about it and couldn't disagree. Which led to another question: How hypocritical is it to not want my grandsons to play a sport that has brought me so much pleasure over the years? I'm still wrestling with that one.

Back when I started, and on through the rest of the last century, the "Big Four" bowl games were the Rose in Pasadena, the Sugar in

New Orleans, and the Cotton in Dallas. The Rose always matched the champions of the Big Ten and Pacific 12 conferences. The Southeastern Conference champion automatically went to the Sugar to play an at-large team. Ditto for the Big 12 Conference in the Orange and the Southwest Conference (now defunct) in the Cotton.

What that meant was that on New Year's Day, several bowls could come into play regarding the national championship. At the end of the 1983 season, for example, unbeaten Nebraska was upset by Miami, which then was ranked sixth or seventh. That vaulted Miami to the national title, something that couldn't happen under the College Football Playoff system that exists today.

I've come to prefer the old way, because more teams had a shot to win the title and there was more drama. Perhaps I'm prejudiced because the old system enabled me to get an *SI* cover story in 1993. Sent to the Sugar Bowl as a precaution in case top-ranked Nebraska was upset in the Orange Bowl, I was ready when *SI* managing editor Mark Mulvoy called and said, "Nebraska got beat, you're on." Miami then defeated Alabama to claim the title, and the next week's magazine had Hurricanes' quarterback Craig Erickson on the cover.

That Alabama team was coached by Bill Curry, who shocked the college football world a few weeks later by giving up the job in Tuscaloosa to take the one at Kentucky, of all places. At the time, I thought UK athletics director C.M. Newton had slammed another home run, just as he had done by talking Rick Pitino into leaving the New York Knicks to take the UK basketball job. Alas, however, it didn't work out for Curry in Lexington. Just when he seemed to be on the brink of turning the corner, some cruel twist of fate, including the murder of a player, would knock him for a loop.

Nevertheless – and maybe I should have mentioned this to my daughter Susan – Curry was as fine a gentleman as I've ever been around in sports. So was his predecessor, Jerry Claiborne, who had a Bryant background similar to Charlie Bradshaw, but conducted himself as a gentleman instead of a tyrant. There are some very good men coaching, football, in other words. I would trust my grandsons to coaches like Claiborne or Curry.

Still, far too many coaches cross the line when it comes to brutality and abuse. They have an inflated view of themselves, which is understandable considering that in 39 of 50 states, the highest-paid public employee is a coach. The more a coach wins, the harder he is to control.

He frequently is more popular than the university president, or even the Governor.

By and large, football coaches also tend to be the worst interviews in sports. At press conferences, they act as if they are prisoners of war being interrogated by the enemy. If clichés were ever outlawed, most of them would have nothing to say. Only rarely do you see a flash of the wit or charm that you get from, say, basketball coaches.

Lee Corso was different. While at Louisville, he once had a turkey lead the team on the field for a Thanksgiving Day game. At Indiana, he once rode into the stadium on an elephant. But for a coach to get away with such shenanigans, he also had better win a lot, which Corso didn't. But when he left coaching, ESPN was waiting for him. The network loved his zany ways, just as they loved Dick Vitale in basketball. And so did Corso go into a new career that earned him a lot more money and recognition than he ever got from coaching.

I still enjoy the games and pageantry, although my pleasure is tempered by thoughts of concussions and other serious injuries. This is a problem that isn't going away — already there's evidence of parents directing their kids to other sports — and the NFL and NCAA had better deal with it instead of pretending it doesn't exist.

But it's easy to put those thoughts on the back burner when the crowd at Michigan is singing "Hail to the Victors Valiant," or when UGA the bulldog is leading Georgia onto the field, or when it's a night game in Baton Rouge and the LSU tiger's amplified growls are whipping up a crowd of 100,000 or so. Nothing beats the pageantry of college football.

I've always liked football players who also were good students, because they help fight the myth that football players are dumber than other students. In 1978, I did a piece for *SI* about Jim Kovach, an outstanding linebacker at Kentucky who also was attending medical school. Oh, yeah. He also was married with a young child. But Kovach pulled it off and spent a few seasons in the NFL before becoming a full-time doctor.

I don't much care who makes the Super Bowl, but I remain interested in who wins Alabama-Auburn, Michigan-Ohio State, or Notre Dame-Southern Cal. It's just in my DNA, I guess. Or maybe it's just what I get for growing up a Cleveland Browns fan. If the sports world has a lost cause today, the poor Browns have to be in the discussion.

A final story to fuel the debate about the value of football:

In the final game of the 1962 season, Bradshaw took his "Thin Thirty" to Knoxville to play Tennessee. At 2-5-2 for the season, Kentucky had nothing at stake except what pride remained after all the publicity over Bradshaw's brutality.

Well, the Cats won, 12-10, on a late field goal by senior Clarkie Mayfield of Black Star, a coal-mining community in Eastern Kentucky. The son of a coal miner, Mayfield refused to let Bradshaw run him off because he didn't want to go back to the mines.

That night I was at Joyland Casino outside Lexington when here came the entire UK team with their dates and wives. Suffice it to say they were feeling no pain now. They even commandeered the stage to sing a boozy version of "On, On U of K."

Now, fast forward to the night of May 28, 1977. Only in his early '30s, Mayfield is the head coach at Jacksonville State University in Alabama. On this night he has reluctantly agreed to join a retirement party for his mother at the Beverly Hills Supper Club outside of Newport.

When a busboy came on stage before featured singer John Davidson and announced that a small fire had started elsewhere in the labyrinth of the building, the crowd started heading toward the exits. But smoke and flames were on them quickly, and an orderly group of about 1,200 turned into a frightened mob, stampeding for the exits that were hard to find.

Mayfield got out with his wife, son, and mother. But others in the 36-person party were still inside. So Mayfield went back in to get them, probably more than once. But he made one trip too many and never came out alive.

A total of 165 perished in the fire, and Mayfield eventually was recognized for doing something far more heroic than anything he ever did on a football field. But the question lingers: Would he have done the same thing had it not been for his football background, especially the hard times under Bradshaw?

All these years later, it's still a question worth debating.

Chapter Thirteen

"CHEER, CHEER FOR OLD NOTRE DAME..."

The walls of the Notre Dame football press box are adorned with framed magazine covers from *Sports Illustrated*, the *Sporting News*, and other national publications. Two of my stories are represented – a cover piece I did for *SI* about quarterback Rick Mirer's first game in 1990, a victory over Michigan, and another about Boston College's upset of the Irish in 1993, only a week after Notre Dame had claimed No. 1 by beating Florida State.

I'm proud of those stories because I've always been fascinated by the mystique of Notre Dame football. Although I was raised a Methodist, my inner Catholic loved the stories about Knute Rockne, The Gipper, The Four Horseman, the national championships, and the Heisman Trophy winners. And then there was that wonderful fight song. I can't decide if Notre Dame or Michigan has the best fight song in college football, so I'm calling it a dead heat.

My first contact with a future Irish legend came in the winter of 1952–53, when I saw the Flaget High basketball team play Ahrens Trade School at Sallie B. Rutherford Elementary, my home from grades three through six. Football All-Staters Paul Hornung and Sherrill Sipes, both bound for South Bend, also played hoops for the Braves. I'm pretty sure I got their autographs after the game.

I didn't make it to Notre Dame until the fall of 1968, only a few months after I had joined the *SI* staff in New York. The Irish were getting ready to host Purdue in an important game, and I was assigned to go to South Bend early in the week and gather material for Dan Jenkins, who may be only the best college football writer ever.

Eager to make an impression, I interviewed Irish coach Ara Parseghian and his players. I attended the Friday night pep rally where actor Pat O'Brien reprised his role of Rockne in the movie about Notre Dame, in which Ronald Reagan, playing George Gipp, told the coach to tell the team to "win one for The Gipper." By the time Jenkins arrived in the press box on game day, I had typed up volumes of notes that I was certain would be the essence of his story.

"Thanks, Billy," said Dan, tossing his notes on the table without even taking a curious riff through them.

The whole game, Jenkins strolled around the press box, chain-smoking (you could do that in those days) and chain-drinking coffee. I never saw him take a note. When the game was over, I worked both locker rooms to get quotes. I hustled back to the press box, typed them up, and gave them to Dan, who said, "Thanks, Billy," and tossed them aside as he resumed typing on his Olivetti portable.

When Dan was done, he handed his copy to a Western Union tele-type operator for transmission to New York. As we left the press box, I noted that Joe Doyle, sports editor of the *South Bend Tribune*, still was working on his story for the next day's edition. I thought I was fast, but Dan put me in the shade.

As you might expect, his story was pure Jenkins — funny, comprehensive, sprinkled with quotes that Dan had gotten just by hanging around, and seamless from beginning to end. I was amazed but also a bit disheartened. His piece was so good, in every respect, that I felt I was in way over my head at *SI*.

Luckily for me, Dan sort of took me under his wing. He introduced me to P.J. Clarke's, then the favored New York watering hole for writers and TV stars. He helped me get assignments, including the 1970 piece on Archie Manning of Ole Miss that was my first *SI* cover. I mainly stayed in the background and marveled about how this dude from Fort Worth, Texas, could bring cowboy cool to New York. His first novel, *Semi-Tough*, was made into a movie starring Burt Reynolds.

Although Dan hasn't written much about college football in many years, I still associate him with Notre Dame. After the 1966 classic against Michigan State, with Notre Dame settling for a 10-10 tie instead of trying to score in the final minutes, Dan began his piece with a play on the Irish fight song: "Old Notre Dame will tie over all." The students in South Bend were so upset that they burned a bunch of magazines in bonfires across campus. I'm sure Dan got a hoot out of that.

Somewhere back in those days, I had an interview with Father Theodore Hesburgh, the president of Notre Dame and a strong voice for the necessity of maintaining balance between athletics and academics.

He convinced me that Notre Dame was a place where doing the right thing always would take precedence over wins and championships. And even though Notre Dame has not been perfect, even though it has been touched by scandal, it seems to be one of the few places that accepts accountability and tries to clean up its messes as honorably as possible.

Indeed, one important reason that Notre Dame hasn't won a national title since 1988 is that the university won't compromise its academic standards for athletes, no matter how talented they may be. This hasn't gone over well with many of the "Subway Alums," the fans from coast-to-coast who cheer for Notre Dame because they're Catholic, even if they have never set foot on campus. (Notre Dame and Boston College are the only Catholic schools that play D-I football). But Notre Dame is not going to budge, and that's another reason I love everything about the place, from The Grotto to "Touchdown Jesus" to the Golden Dome.

I also should mention that Notre Dame has been blessed with some of the best and most effective sports information directors in the nation. Although Notre Dame was only 2-8 in Hornung's senior year, Charley Callahan worked miracles to get him the 1956 Heisman Trophy, the only time a player from a losing team has won it. Roger Valdiserri convinced Joe Theismann to change the pronunciation of his name, so it would rhyme with Heisman. And John Heisler continues to run one of the most professional and accommodating operations in the country.

Somewhere in 2004, Hornung approached me about being his ghost writer on a book about his career. Besides football, the publisher, Simon-Schuster, wanted to know about the gambling that got him banned from the NFL for a year and the other elements of his playboy lifestyle (the women, in other words). Paul originally had asked the famed Dick Schaap to do the book with him, but Dick, also a friend of mine, had died unexpectedly.

Paul and I had gotten to be friends because, as sports editor of the *C-J*, I had campaigned for him to be inducted into the Pro Football Hall of Fame, which was keeping him out due to his gambling ban. I also testified for Paul at a trial in which he had sued WTBS in Atlanta for refusing to hire him as an analyst because of the gambling. Mainly, though, his mother liked what I wrote about him, and Paul worshipped his mother.

Our book got positive reviews just about everywhere except South Bend, where the priests and nuns were shocked by Paul's revelation that he had gotten a girl pregnant before his senior year at Notre Dame. He said he told the girl to keep it quiet, which she did. Later, she also told him that she had "taken care of it," which could mean only one thing. He said they went out a couple more times, but "it was never the same."

I became a Roman Catholic sometime after that, and I swear that the book and Notre Dame football had nothing to do with it. I simply went to Mass a few times with a friend, Martha McMahon, and something took. I can't explain it, so I won't try. But I felt that a hole in my heart had been filled, and I came to know a feeling of peace that I had never known.

I didn't expect that my conversion would have a sports twist, but it did. A few years after I joined the church, my friend Paul Najjar introduced me to Steve Fehder, a former radio executive who was starting a business called the Louisville Catholic Sports Network. I signed on as Executive Editor, and together, Steve and I have developed several projects, most notably the Louisville Catholic Sports Hall of Fame. Many of the inductees have told me our Hall of Fame was more important to them than bigger and better-known ones because ours is about home, family, and values. I like that.

Although Louisville has a large Catholic population, a surprisingly small number of the best players from Trinity, St. Xavier, and the other Catholic schools have played at Notre Dame. I'm not sure why because the Louisville chapter of the Notre Dame Alumni Association always has been active in promoting the university. Nevertheless, Louisville has hardly been a pipeline to South Bend.

One of college sports' big mysteries, at least to me, is why Notre hasn't been more successful in men's basketball. Despite a history that includes the names of such great players as Tom Hawkins, Adrian Dantley, Austin Carr, David Rivers, and others, Notre Dame's only trip to the Final Four came in 1978, when they lost to Coach Bill Foster's young Duke team in the semifinals (Duke lost to UK in the title game).

Even now, Notre Dame basketball is best known for its 1973 upset of UCLA in South Bend, ending the Bruins' eighty-eight-game winning streak. But that's a long time ago, and it would seem the Irish are overdue for a major breakout, especially with ex-Duke assistant Mike Brey sitting in the chair once occupied by the flamboyant Digger Phelps.

If you dig deep enough into the history of Notre Dame basketball, you'll find that Hornung was a member of the varsity in 1954–55, his sophomore year. Irish football coach Terry Brennan let basketball coach Johnny Jordan borrow him, and he acquitted himself well, averaging 6.1 points for a 14-10 team, with a career high of 13 against DePaul.

Hornung told me about it for our book.

"Jordan liked to tip a few," he said, "and sometimes, on the road, he'd take me out drinking with him. He could do that because I wasn't on a basketball scholarship. I earned my monogram, but never played basketball again because Brennan was afraid I'd neglect my studies and become academically ineligible for football."

While I'm on the subject of Catholic sports, I should mention that I'm proud of the "Little Notre Dame" we have in Louisville.

I liked Bellarmine University basketball when my friends Jim Spalding and Joe Reibel were running the program there. But it wasn't until 2012 that I really became a regular at Knights' Hall on the NCAA Division II school's campus.

I went to a Knights' game to support Scotty Davenport, a friend who coached the basketball team at Ballard High when my daughters Amy and Susan were students there in the late 1980s. From there, Scotty joined Denny Crum's staff at U of L, and Rick Pitino kept him when he succeeded Crum in 2002.

Scotty and the Bellarmine job were perfect for each other. He got the chance to become a college head coach at a place that shared his values, and the university got a high-energy, hard-working coach who had the personality to recruit and win new fans.

That first time I saw Scotty's team play, I felt at home. A small, liberal arts school, Bellarmine reminded me a lot of my alma mater, Transylvania University. It was a place where the balance between academics and athletics was carefully maintained. But, mostly, Scotty's team played the game the way I thought it should be played. The Knights did not depend on athleticism, as most D-I teams do these days, but on hustle, teamwork, ball-handling, passing, and finding the open man.

I became so enthused that when Bob Knight, retired from coaching and working as an analyst for ESPN, came to Louisville for a Cardinals' game in 2013, I asked that he let me take him to Knights' Hall, so he could talk to the team, then a serious contender for the D-II national title.

"Bob," I said, "you'll love them. They play the game the way you used to coach it. And their players graduate, just as yours always did."

Well, the players were on the floor, shooting around, when we walked in the gym, and I'll never forget the stunned look on their faces when they saw Knight. After greeting Knight, Scotty ordered his players into the locker room, where Knight talked to them for about twenty minutes before posing with the team for a photo.

A few weeks later, after Bellarmine won the national championship in Springfield, Massachusetts, Knight called to ask me to congratulate the team and tell Scotty he had watched the semifinals and finals on CBS.

To this day, I'm a Bellarmine season-ticket holder. Scotty has allowed me to come to practice and be in the locker room before games, for which I'm very grateful. Every time I see the Knights play, it reminds me of everything I've always loved about basketball.

Chapter Fourteen

THE ART OF INTERVIEWING

In my experience, the best journalists also are the best interviewers. They have an innate ability to get subjects to trust them. They earn that trust by being open-minded, responsible, prepared, and insightful.

Back in the day, getting access to news sources was so much easier than it is now. When I was covering University of Kentucky basketball for the *Courier-Journal* in 1967 and '68, I sometimes would drop by Coach Adolph Rupp's office without having made an appointment. Ms. Louise Gilchrest was his assistant and gatekeeper, and usually the door was open between her office and Coach Rupp's.

"Ms. Gilchrist," I would say, "if Coach Rupp is in, I'd like to ask him a couple of questions."

"Coach," she would say, leaning back in her chair, "Billy Reed is here, and he'd like to see you for a minute."

Then would come Coach Rupp's voice in that famed Kansas nasal twang of his.

"What does that little turd want now? Tell him to come on in."

To get a few one-on-one minutes with a high-profile coach today, you must fight through layers of assistants, sports information people, and personal assistants, most of whom regard you with suspicion and disdain. I think it would be easier to get an audience with the Pope than, say, Mike Krzyzewski. In today's world of multi-million-dollar contracts, coaches at the biggest programs are more CEOs than teachers of basketball or football.

There is an art to being a good interviewer. It helps to have a friendly personality. It's essential to know some background about your subject. If you have a tidbit of information that you can use as an ice-breaker that will put the subject at ease, so much the better.

Before I interviewed John Swofford, commissioner of the Atlantic Coast Conference, for *Conversations with Champions*, the show I do for Kentucky Educational Television, I noticed in one of his profiles that he had an older brother who was a popular singer in the late 1960s and early '70s.

Working under the name "Oliver," his biggest hit was "Good Morning, Starshine," from the hit Broadway play *Hair*. When I mentioned this to Swofford early in our interview, he lit up with happiness and told me about a summer when he toured the nation with his brother, working as one of his "roadies." He said it was the best summer of his life.

The rest of the interview went beautifully, at least partly because my question about his brother had caused him to relax and told him that I had done my homework.

Honesty is vital to a good interview. If a subject asks if he or she can tell you something off the record and you promise to do so, you had better live up to that promise if you care about your reputation. It's also important to treat subjects differently, according to their age. For example, I always have treated high school athletes differently than professionals, taking into account their immaturity and inexperience.

Sometimes you get good stuff from a subject but wonder whether to use it. In 1977, after UK's second football game of the season, senior quarterback Derrick Ramsey, an African American, was booed by the crowd in Commonwealth Stadium. As he undressed in the locker room, a visibly angry Ramsey implied that racism was behind at least some of the booing.

I knew that if I wrote my *C-J* column about his comments, both he and I would be in trouble with the Big Blue fan base. But I also knew that if I didn't use them, Derrick might not respect me and figure I was just another part of the problem. I finally decided that if he had the courage to say what he did, I had the courage to print it.

Unsurprisingly, I got a phone call that Sunday from UK Coach Fran Curci. He was upset that I had used the quotes and accused me of taking advantage of Derrick before he had cooled off. But Derrick, to his eternal credit, stood by what he said. His teammates rallied around him, and the Wildcats didn't lose another game, finishing 10-1 and sixth in the national polls.

About five years before that, *Sports Illustrated* sent me to Los Angeles to do a cover story on Bill Walton, the 6-foot-11 sophomore basketball sensation at UCLA. When I checked in with the sports information office, I was surprised to learn that Walton didn't want to talk with me. Puzzled, I asked to meet Walton, so he could at least tell me what was wrong.

"Last week *Sports Illustrated* had a story about (Ole Miss star) Johnny Neumann," Walton said. "The first part of it was all about his zits (acne), and it made him look silly. I have a stuttering problem. How do I know you won't do that same thing to me?"

It was a reasonable question. The author of the Neumann piece was Curry Kirkpatrick, a gifted writer whose trademark was being as outrageous as possible. I told Walton that although Curry and I worked for the same magazine, we viewed a lot of things differently. I told him that I had never made fun of anybody's looks or impediments.

Walton decided to take a chance, and we hit it off well. He took me to San Diego to have dinner with his parents. He also told me some off-the-record stuff about UCLA that I agreed to keep between the two of us. I'm sure Curry could have written a more, ah, colorful story than mine, but I was pleased with the piece and so, from what I heard, was Bill's family.

Another time Curry wanted to do a piece about Lawrence Funderburke, a talented-but-troubled player who had transferred from Bob Knight's alma mater, Ohio State, into the coach's program at Indiana. It was a big controversy at the time, and Curry wanted to put his spin on it. But Knight said he would agree to co-operate only if Curry wrote about the entire team and not just Funderburke. He also said he didn't want Curry to use a tape recorder.

Curry agreed, but he had no intention of abiding by the guidelines. He sat down in Assembly Hall and interviewed the IU players one-by-one. Every interview was more or less the same. After a few perfunctory questions about the team, Curry would bring up Funderburke. The process ended when a tape recorder fell out of Curry's pocket and clattered to the floor.

A good sports information director, such as Kenny Klein at the University of Louisville, can facilitate the interviewing process immeasurably. He can tell both the writer and the subject what to expect from each other. If a problem arises, he can act as a mediator if he has the trust and confidence of both parties.

When Digger Phelps was coaching basketball at Notre Dame, he got upset with me for doing a piece about his losing record against UK in Freedom Hall. That piece ran before a meeting between the two, and when Notre Dame secured a rare victory over UK, Digger came charging across the floor and got in my face. "This one was for you," he said, jabbing his finger at me. "For you!" And then he whirled around and headed for the locker room.

In a follow-up column, I wrote that if Notre Dame had won the game for me, the least Digger could do was send me the game ball. A few days later, a package from South Bend was delivered to my office at the *C-J*. Inside was an ancient basketball with the score of the UK-Notre Dame on it and a nice note from Digger.

I could see the fine hand of Roger Valdiserri, Notre Dame's iconic sports information director, at work. He probably told Digger he had over-reacted to my column and needed to do something to make light of it. Whatever happened, Digger and I got along well after that.

Today coaches prefer to deal with the media mostly through press conferences, which generally produce little or nothing of news value. When you have newspaper writers, radio and TV personalities, bloggers, podcasters, and fan-show homers trying to pursue their vastly different agendas, it's impossible to ask follow-up questions or pursue a specific train of thought.

Of all the beat writers I've ever worked with or against, the most fearless interviewer was Jerry Tipton of the *Lexington Herald-Leader*. Although UK basketball coaches and fans wanted him to be a Wildcat homer, Jerry remained a professional journalist who always asked the tough questions that others were too intimidated to ask.

That's why I always trusted Jerry's stories and columns. He only wanted to report the truth, regardless of the reaction he might get. He kept his personal feelings to himself. Although many in the Big Blue fan base hated him for doing his job professionally, I suspect that most of the UK coaches secretly respected him for holding them accountable for their words and deeds. At least, I hope that's the case.

I got a lot of good interviews as a member in good standing of the SEC "Skywriters." This was a novel concept that was good for both coaches and the media. A few weeks before the start of football season, the "Skywriters," a motley collection of writers and broadcasters, would gather in Birmingham. The next morning we would board a two-engine DC-3 of World War II vintage and begin a five-day odyssey in which we would visit every training camp in the league.

Besides getting stuff for the next day's paper, you could stock up on material that could be used throughout the season. And at each hotel where we stayed, the SEC would sponsor a hospitality room where coaches could drop in after practice, if they wished, and socialize with the media off the record. I remember that Johnny Majors of Tennessee was not adverse to drinking a little whiskey and playing poker.

Those days are long gone, of course, and it's mostly because of the corporate mentality that has taken over big-time college athletics. It's also because of the rise of social media at the same time newspapers are dying or declining. Coaches no longer need writers to burnish their images or get out their messages, so they focus on radio and TV, where they get paid to do shows, and on social media, which allows them to speak directly to the public without a media filter.

It's also gotten harder to interview players at every level. Some, of course, are so inarticulate that they're not worth interviewing. But the majority of them have been schooled from a young age to be wary of the media and say as little as possible. But the coaches have yet to figured out how to control players' Twitter and Facebook accounts. If a player today says anything inflammatory, controversial, or revealing, it will be more likely found on social media than in the local newspaper.

The hardest interviews come after a coach or player has been accused of NCAA rules infractions or even crimes. Many times, a journalist has been around the accused party long enough to regard him or her as a friend, so it's difficult to shift gears. The reporter claims to only be doing his or her job. The accused party retorts that the reporter is betraying their friendship and should be a defender instead of an interrogator.

For example, when Eddie Sutton was accused of NCAA rules violations while coaching the UK basketball team, he initially refused to do in-depth interviews. He finally relented but would only talk to me. So, I made arrangements for a *Herald-Leader* photographer and myself to sit down with Eddie and his wife Patsy in their home.

For me, it was a tough couple of hours. I liked Eddie, and I appreciated the compliment he paid me by singling me out to do the interview. Still, I had to ask all the tough questions. I wasn't sure if he was lying to save his job and reputation or whether he was telling me the truth as best he could.

Back at the office, editor John Carroll and I decided I should write the interview as a straight news story, without any editorial comment, and I'm confident that was the right way to go.

Chapter Fifteen

BEWARE THE BULLY PULPIT

Every sports columnist worth his or her weight in press box hot dogs should have at least one great crusade in his or her career. In my case, I used my bully pulpit to campaign against the University of Kentucky's obstinate refusal to schedule a regular-season basketball series against the University of Louisville.

I suppose I was successful. At least, Earl Cox, my longtime friend and colleague, said that the two people who did the most to make it happen were John Y. Brown Jr., the Commonwealth's governor from 1979–83, and yours truly. I appreciated that, especially since it was Earl who told me in the beginning, "Billy, that series is never going to happen in my lifetime."

In fairness to Earl, some background is in order.

When Adolph Rupp came to UK in 1930, neither the NCAA nor the Southeastern Conference existed. College football was huge, but basketball was only something to do in the wintertime. It wasn't uncommon for UK to play other state schools, including Transylvania, Centre, and Georgetown.

But Rupp changed all that. Noting that basketball was becoming popular in the Northeast, he took his team to play in New York's Madison Square Garden every chance he got. When the SEC was founded in 1933, he began playing a different kind of schedule. The first NCAA tournament in 1939 gave him a national goal for which to shoot. Rupp made UK supreme among the state's colleges, and he saw nothing to gain and something to lose by playing them.

But U of L began to break away from the pack in 1948, winning the NAIB championship over Indiana State and a coach named John Wooden. The Cardinals followed that by winning the championship of the 1956 National Invitation Tournament, which was then almost as prestigious as the NCAA event. And in 1959, Rupp's worst nightmare came true when Peck Hickman's Cardinals upset UK's defending national champions in the semis of the Mideast Regional. A victory over Iowa in the title game enabled them to go back home to Freedom Hall for their first NCAA Final Four appearance.

Probably the most important player in the histories of both programs was Wes Unseld, the 6-foot-6 star who led Louisville Seneca High to back-to-back state titles in 1963 and '64. During Unseld's senior season, UK President John Oswald and Governor Ed Breathitt were working behind the scenes for Rupp to integrate his program, even if it meant leaving the SEC. Unseld would have been the perfect pioneer — excellent player, good student, model citizen.

Rupp, indeed, offered Unseld a scholarship after the 1964 season. Had Unseld accepted it, he would have been the center on the beloved "Rupp's Runts" team of 1965–66 instead of Thad Jaracz, and the trajectory of UK basketball would have been changed forever. However, Unseld declined UK's offer when the coach told his mother that he could not absolutely guarantee her son's safety when UK went on the road in the Deep South, where the Ku Klux Klan was riding high.

So, Unseld went to U of L, which changed that program forever. Although he never made it to the Final Four in his three varsity years, Unseld and the talented Butch Beard, who was a year younger, made the Cards a fixture on the national radar screen.

Still, all was relatively quiet on the UK-U of L front until 1971, when U of L hired Denny Crum away from John Wooden's side at UCLA. Crum's first season at U of L coincided with Rupp's last season at UK, and his parting gift to Rupp was a lot of heartburn. Not only did Crum refuse to accept UK's superiority in the state, but he also called for a series between the two programs and said he had two freshmen, Junior Bridgeman and Allen Murphy, who were better than any of UK's vaunted recruiting class of Mr. Basketballs from four states — Jimmy Dan Conner from Kentucky, Mike Flynn from Indiana, Kevin Grevey from Ohio, and Bob Guyette from Illinois.

Well, now. Just who did this loudmouth from UCLA think he was, challenging mighty UK so audaciously?

In 1975, as fate would have it, the teams almost met for the national championship. Both had made it to the Final Four in San Diego — the Wildcats had upset unbeaten Indiana in the Mideast Regional Final — and both were favored to win their semifinal games. UK did its part by handling Syracuse, but Crum and U of L were upset by, of all people, John Wooden and UCLA. Disappointed Cardinal fans were mollified a bit when the Bruins beat UK in the championship game, after which Wooden rode off into the history books with ten titles in his final twelve years at UCLA.

When I became sports editor of the *Courier-Journal* in May 1977, I knew Joe B. Hall, Rupp's successor, better than Crum and had no particular axe to grind about a basketball series. But when U of L won the school its first NCAA title in 1980, I really began to push hard, which earned me the cold shoulder from Hall and the wrath of his huge fan base.

The day of the NCAA title game in Indianapolis, I was looking for something to write for the *C-J's* first edition, which would go to press before the U of L-UCLA title game. I always tried to do my best by our readers in the far reaches of the Commonwealth. So, I figured, no matter whether U of L won or lost, the time had come for the series to happen, and I wrote as much in a column that was printed in all four editions. I can only imagine the reactions of Big Blue diehards in, say, Pikeville or Paducah when they opened their papers and found no game column from me, only one pushing UK to schedule U of L.

That started a three-year period of controversy that Hall's stubbornness turned into a national story. He claimed that Coach Rupp had a policy of not scheduling other schools in the state, and he was only honoring that policy. But that also was a thinly-veiled insult to U of L, who had long surpassed Western Kentucky, Eastern, Morehead, and Murray State on the national stage.

I was the first sports editor of the *C-J* to regularly take on the UK basketball coach. Hall's response was to freeze me out and try to deny me access to his program. My counter-response was to ram Denny Crum and Bobby Knight down his throat. During this period of conflict, I wrote a column about Hall's program using quotes from George Orwell's *1984*, a novel about a totalitarian state. When Hall was asked about it, he said, with a straight face, "I always thought Orwell was a good writer." It was one of the better lines of his career.

In the 1982 Mideast Regional, it looked as if UK and U of L were destined to play in the regional semifinals. However, that was foiled when the Wildcats were shocked by Middle Tennessee State in a preregional game in Nashville. Asked what happened, Hall said his players had lost "their electrolytes," whatever that meant. UK's case for not scheduling U of L suffered more damage when the Cardinals made it to the Final Four in New Orleans, where they lost to Patrick Ewing and Georgetown in the national semifinals.

But in the next season's tournament, the historic matchup finally took place in Knoxville, Tennessee. The field for the Mideast Regional was Kentucky, Louisville, Indiana, and Arkansas. After eliminating the Hoosiers in the first semifinals, Hall and his team took seats in the stands to watch U of L-Arkansas. It looked as if the Razorbacks might be spoilers, but a last-second tip-in by U of L's Scooter McCray pulled out a win for Crum's team and created the first UK-U of L matchup since Peck Hickman's Cardinals had upset the Cats in the 1959 Mideast Regional.

The day before the game, Hall had the misfortune of doing his press conference before Crum. Dour and defensive, Hall repeated the same old tired reasons for not scheduling the Cards in the regular season. Crum followed with what may have been the best press conference of his career. He was witty, charming, loose, and sarcastic. Had somebody been keeping score, it would have been a blowout for Crum.

That's how I wrote it for my game day column in the *C-J*, and the editors devoted the entire front page to it. At the end, I also picked U of L to win by 12. Since the *C-J* sent trucks of papers to Knoxville, all the fans of both teams knew about my column and prediction by mid-morning. I did not think it a good sign when David Hawpe, the *C-J* managing editor and a staunch UK fan, turned his back when he saw me in the hotel lobby.

I got heckled loudly by Big Blue supporters as I took my press table seat before the game, and I got heckled again when I went to the press hospitality room at halftime. The Wildcats held a seven-point lead at the intermission, and the UK faithful wanted to remind me of my prediction in the loudest possible way.

The second half was about as taut as taut gets. Back and forth, up and down, live or die. The Cats sent it into overtime when Jim Master hit a short jumper off the glass with only seconds remaining. It might have been better for the Cats if he had missed because the Cards, led by ball-hawking guards Lancaster Gordon and Milt Wagner, owned the OT. When the final horn sound, the Cards had won by 80-68. Or 12 points, exactly as I had predicted. As I walked off the floor, my Big Blue hecklers had disappeared.

As Hall was talking to the media, I was standing at the side of the room when I felt someone grab the sleeve of my sport coat and twist it. Turning, I looked into the angry eyes of Joe's wife Katharine. "You've ruined one of the finest men who ever lived," she hissed. "You're nothing but an ass-kisser for Bobby Knight and Denny Crum."

While I was still digesting that, Crum moved up on my other side and whispered, "Sorry about that overtime, Bill." He was smiling hugely and chewing gum rapidly. Finally, his dogged insistence that his program was as good as UK's had been vindicated.

A few days after the Final Four, where the Cards were defeated by Houston's "Phi Slamma Jamma" team in a rim-rattling semifinal, UK waved the white flag. Under pressure from President Otis Singletary, who knew the PR battle had been lost, the Board of Trustees ordered Athletics Director Cliff Hagan to begin negotiations with U of L for a regular-season series.

It began that December in Rupp Arena with 7-foot Sam Bowie leading the Cats to a 70-44 victory that made the cover of *Sports Illustrated*. It continues to this day, and there is not a shred of evidence that UK has lost a single fan to U of L or that the Cards have made serious inroads on UK's grip on the state. The series has provided great basketball and entertainment for both the Commonwealth and the nation. While at UK, Rick Pitino dominated Crum every bit as much as John Calipari dominated him in the last eight years of his tenure at Louisville.

But I must add a cautionary tale about the power of the bully pulpit.

In 1969, Coach Rupp integrated UK's program by signing Tom Payne, a 7-foot-2 center from Louisville Shawnee. Since freshmen were ineligible for varsity play in those days, Payne played at UK only as a sophomore in 1970–71 before moving to the NBA's Atlanta Hawks as what was then known as a "hardship" case, meaning he needed the money to support himself and his family.

While with the Hawks, Payne was charged with numerous rapes in the Atlanta area, was convicted, and went to prison. His mother believed he was being framed by Georgia police departments because he was black and began a movement called "Drum Major for Justice." When she came to me to solicit some public support, I read the cases and agreed that she might have a point. In one case, for example, the assailant supposedly raped his victim in the backseat of a Volkswagen. I had a hard time imagining that one.

When Payne was transferred to the Jefferson County jail in Louisville, my friend Dave Kindred and I arranged an interview with him. Physically, he was awesome, not a pound of fat on him and his broad shoulders tapering to a small waist. He also was soft-spoken, seemed contrite, and said he would make the best of another chance.

Being the bleeding-heart liberal that I am, I wrote a column that was sympathetic to Payne. I also called a friend who was on the state parole board and said I believed he had learned his lesson and would not be a threat if set free. Well, Payne got his parole. For a few months, he played for a local minor-league pro team named the Catbirds. Then he went to California and, next thing I heard, he was back in jail for more rapes.

That both saddened me and shook me up. I had misjudged Payne badly. Obviously, he had a disease that I was totally unqualified to see, much less diagnose. It bothered me that I had used my bully pulpit to more or less endorse his release from jail.

Never again did I get involved in a criminal case unless I was absolutely, positively sure, beyond a reasonable doubt, of the accused's guilt or innocence. A columnist is only as good as his reputation for seeing and telling the truth, and this time I had failed my readers and myself.

Chapter Sixteen

CONFESSIONS OF A
CIVIC BOOSTER

I deally, a journalist is not supposed to be a "homer" or civic booster. But sometimes, when you're a sports editor in a mid-level city like Louisville, you have to bend the rules of journalism just a bit in order to support something you believe will be good for the community in which you live, work, worship, and play.

I wasn't the first to feel that way. Earl Ruby, the *C-J's* sports editor from the 1930s to 1969, was active in community affairs. He helped start the Kentucky Derby Festival and the Kentucky Athletic Hall of Fame.

When I got Ruby's old job in 1977, after stints by Dean Eagle and Dave Kindred, I quickly discovered a band of brothers who all felt it was their duty to help promote their cities. I'm talking about sports editors and columnists such as Bill Millsaps of Richmond (Virginia), George Lapides of Memphis, Hubert Mizell of St. Petersburg, Bill Bibb of Nashville, Freddie Russell of Nashville, Si Burick of Dayton, Tom McEwen of Tampa, Dan Foster of Greensville (South Carolina), and many more.

They all loved their cities but not so much that they would sacrifice their journalistic integrity. It's a delicate balancing act, and I was asked to walk my own tightrope in 1981, when I got a phone call from banker Dan Ulmer, asking me to meet him to talk about bringing professional Triple-A baseball back to Louisville after a ten-year absence.

I was immediately intrigued because professional baseball was part of Louisville's DNA. Back in the late 1800s, we had a team in the major leagues. That was about the same time that Hillerich & Bradsby began making the bats that would make "Louisville Slugger" an iconic international brand.

In the late 1930s, a local kid named Pee Wee Reese played shortstop for the Louisville Colonels before eventually winding up in Brooklyn, where he became captain of the Dodgers' immortal "Boys of Summer" teams that included Jackie Robinson, Duke Snider, Roy Campanella, and other future Hall of Famers.

In the early 1950s, when I was in elementary school, the Colonels were the top farm team of the Boston Red Sox, and I became a member of their "Knothole Gang," so named because of the Norman Rockwell image of kids peeping through knotholes in wooden fences to watch baseball games.

My favorite Colonels' player was Harry Agganis, a former All-American quarterback at Boston University who decided to play pro baseball instead of football. A hard-hitting first-baseman, Agganis spent only a summer in Louisville before moving up to Boston. After his last game at Parkway Field, next door to the University of Louisville, he brought a broken bat out of the clubhouse and gave it to the nearest kid, which happened to be me.

I followed Harry religiously in the *Courier-Journal* and the *Sporting News*. He seemed well on the way to stardom when he became gravely ill and died. It was my first encounter with man's mortality, and I was stunned. How could death come so quickly to a man so young and apparently healthy?

The Colonels remained a fixture in Louisville, despite various changes in owners and parent clubs, until 1972, when Lee Corso, of all people, played a major role in running them out of town.

Back then, Corso was U of L's head football coach, and the fans loved him for the same reasons he has amassed such a following as a co-host of ESPN's *GameDay* college football show. He was funny, clever, and unpredictable. When his 1971 team went 9-1 and played in the Pasadena Bowl, he pretty much owned the city. So, when he complained about the swamp that the Cardinal Stadium football field became every time it rained, the State Fair Board agreed to get rid of the grass and replace it with artificial turf.

But this so angered Bill Gardner, the owner of the Colonels, that he moved his franchise to Pawtucket, Rhode Island, where it still exists as a Red Sox Triple-A farm team. Adding insult to injury, Corso also pulled up stakes, taking the head coaching job at Indiana University. So, Louisville was left without Corso and without Triple-A baseball but with a new artificial field.

During the next decade, the city spent its summers without professional baseball. Fortunately, that was the glory era of the "Big Red Machine" in Cincinnati, so many Louisvillians adopted the Reds as their team and made countless trips up Interstate 71 to Riverfront Stadium. Still, it wasn't the same as having your own home team.

When I met with Dan Ulmer, he told me that he had been in discussions with a fellow named A. Ray Smith about moving the St. Louis Cardinals Triple-A team from Springfield, Illinois, to Louisville. He said Smith wanted to come but needed to talk to various community leaders, including the sports editor of the *C-J*. Eagerly, I agreed to meet Smith and hear him out.

Smith was the shrewdest promoter to hit Louisville since Col. Matt Winn turned the Kentucky Derby into the world's most famous Thoroughbred race. He tried to come off as an "ol' country boy" from Oklahoma, but all you had to do was look into his blue eyes to see a shrewd businessman. The first question he asked me was "Are you a baseball man?"

I knew exactly what he meant. He wanted to know if I liked baseball and would make sure his team received its fair share of space and coverage. I assured him that I had loved baseball all my life, going back to the days when I collected cards, played sandlot games in the South End, and was a teammate of Mitch McConnell on the Giants of the Beechmont Pony League. I told him we would make his team, the Redbirds, our major beat in the summer. However, I also told him that we wouldn't be "homers," that we would report on the bad news as well as the good.

That seemed to satisfy him, and we became good friends. When he decided to bring the Redbirds to Louisville, I felt a little guilty about the fans in Springfield, who had supported the team well. But the guilt was overridden by the pride of helping to bring something to my city that would enhance our quality of life.

The story turned out to be huge. In 1982, the Redbirds' first summer here, the franchise broke the all-time minor-league attendance record. The next season, the Redbirds became the first minor-league team to surpass one million in home attendance. Nobody was surprised when the millionth fan to walk through the turnstiles was A. Ray's barber. As I said, the man was a promotional genius.

In 1986, A. Ray sold the team to a group of local investors, headed by Ulmer, and returned to Oklahoma with "Miss Alice," his longtime assistant. I missed our good times together. One evening, as both of us were being overserved in Hasenour's Restaurant, we agreed that A. Ray would buy the Cincinnati Reds and make me his general manager. At the time, it seemed like an inspired idea. The next morning, it didn't make as much sense. We never spoke of it again.

As fate would have it, the Redbirds' first season in Louisville coincided with the parent team in St. Louis winning the National League pennant. That made covering the World Series special for me because I had gotten to know several of the players and Cardinals' manager Whitey Herzog.

One morning during the games in St. Louis, A. Ray called my motel room and asked if I would like to have brunch at Stan Musial's home. I was shocked. Stan the Man? One of the game's all-time greatest players? Was he serious?

A couple of hours later, I met A. Ray and his good friend William H. May, who had been chairman of the Kentucky State Racing Commission when Jim Bolus and I did our investigation of fixed races. He and I had grown to be friends. I admired Mr. May's keen mind and ability to cut through complex issues.

Next thing I know, I was shaking hands with Stan Musial in the foyer of his home. I don't remember much about it because, even at my age, I was awed to be in the presence of one of baseball's all-time greats. At one point, Musial played the harmonica while everyone sang "Take Me Out to the Ball Game."

To this day, whenever I go to a Louisville Bats game in the wonderful downtown park on the banks of the Ohio River, I think about A. Ray and the fun we had. He seemed to know everybody in baseball. One day, over lunch at Hasenour's, we began talking about Keith Hernandez of the Mets, and Smith immediately got him on the phone.

Only a couple of years later, I again found myself in the awkward position of using my position to help city officials make Louisville a better sports town. This time I think it was former Gov. John Y. Brown Jr. who enlisted my support. He wanted to bring in Howard Schnellenberger to coach the University of Louisville football team.

A native of St. Meinrad, Indiana, Schnellenberger had played his high school ball at Flaget High in west Louisville. His coach was Paulie Miller and his teammates included Paul Hornung, who won the 1956 Heisman Trophy at Notre Dame. Schnellenberger went to UK to play for Coach Paul "Bear" Bryant, but Bryant suddenly left Lexington for Texas A&M shortly after Schnellenberger's sophomore season.

Schnellenberger spent his last two seasons playing for Blanton Collier, then embarked on a coaching career that earned him national championship rings with Bryant at Alabama, Super Bowl rings with Don Shula of the Miami Dolphins, and another national championship ring as head coach of the Miami Hurricanes, who won the 1983 title with a stunning upset of mighty Nebraska in the Orange Bowl.

Unfortunately, Schnellenberger left Miami for the fledgling United States Football League but was left without a job when his franchise folded. Nevertheless, he still was the nation's hottest coaching property when Brown, Dan Ulmer, U of L athletics director Bill Olsen, and others began calling him about the U of L job.

At first, Schnellenberger dismissed the idea out of hand. But the people in Louisville were so persistent that he started to listen. With every conversation, they sweetened the pot. Several talked to me on an off-the-record basis and began telling me that it was going to happen, that Schnellenberger was going to come, so that's the way I wrote it in my column.

One morning Earl Cox, my former boss and current colleague, came into my office and shut the door. "Billy, stop writing that s—t," he said. "You're making yourself look bad." I told him I trusted my sources and he left, shaking his head in frustration. But guess what? It did happen. Schnellenberger came to U of L, vowing to turn the Cardinals into a Top 25 program. "Louisville is on a collision course with the national championship," he said in that gruff, hyperbolic way of his. "The only variable is time."

And that was the beginning of the rise of U of L football. By the time Schnellenberger left after the 1995 season, he owned a bowl victory over Alabama and the knowledge that he had, indeed, started the program on the path to the great victories forged by successors such as John L. Smith, Bobby Petrino, and Charlie Strong. In 2016, Cards quarterback Lamar Jackson won the Heisman Trophy, which was unthinkable in Louisville before Schnellenberger.

In my role as civic do-gooder, I also had an idea for my friend Paul Hornung that came to fruition, although in a way that still puzzles me.

In the fall of 2006, Notre Dame devoted one of its home games to honoring Paul, the university's 1956 Heisman Trophy winner. Paul rented a bus and invited a few friends, including me, to go with him to South Bend and share in the festivities. It was a memorable experience, especially the moment during the Friday night pep rally when Paul's pants slipped to his knees as he was talking to the crowd, which gasped and then erupted in laughter. It seems Paul had recently lost some weight and forgot his belt.

On the way home, for some odd reason, I got an idea. Since Paul was known for his versatility — he ran, passed, caught passes, place-kicked, and played defense at Notre Dame — why not establish a national award in his name that would go to the most versatile player in college football? The award would be presented every year in Louisville, which would help the city's econ .ny and image.

As the bus rolled along, I mentioned my idea to a couple of Paul's other friends. They loved it and promised to support it. So, then I went to the front of the bus, where Paul was wolfing down a cheeseburger, and told him about it. I'll never forget his response. "Aw, that's what college football needs," he said. "Another f-----g award." That let the air out of that balloon, and I didn't think about it again until a couple of years later, when I was driving home after teaching a class at Indiana University.

The radio was tuned to WHAS840 in Louisville, and suddenly I heard the news that the Louisville Sports Commission had announced it was going to sponsor an award in honor of Paul Hornung that would go to the most versatile player in college football. It was my idea, exactly, and I was so surprised I almost drove my car off the road. But something else had been added to our sports menu and how it happened really doesn't matter.

Finally, I'm sure everyone is aware that Louisville now is known as "The Ville," but let me tell you how that happened.

Before the championship season of 1979–80, I covered a U of L scrimmage in Charlestown, Indiana. After the game, in the crowded locker room, I heard Poncho Wright, a valuable reserve and native of Indianapolis, shouting, "The Ville's going to the 'Nap, the Ville's going to the 'Nap."

When I asked Poncho for a translation, he told me he was saying that "The Ville," as in Louisville, was going to "the 'Nap," as in Indianapolis, for the 1980 Final Four. I put that in my column, and I'm pretty sure it was the first time "The Ville" was ever used in print.

Over the years, I've told Poncho it's too bad we didn't trademark the phrase because today we would be rich men.

Chapter Seventeen

FATHERS AND SONS

I don't think being a good parent has anything to do with race, religion, or status in life, but I believe it has everything to do with love and unselfishness. The problem with loving a job as much as I did mine is that it can throw your life out of balance if you let it. Nothing in life is more important, or more complicated, than being a parent.

It becomes even more complicated when parents have a precocious son or daughter. From what I've seen, that can bring out the best — or, more frequently, the worst — in a parent. I'm talking about the parents who want to relive their lives through their kids, who expect them to be their meal tickets, or who teach them that money is more important than education or simple decency.

The first father-son relationship that really intrigued me was the one between basketball coach Press Maravich and his son Pete, the all-time leading scorer in college hoops.

An intense man of Serbian ancestry, Press was a good enough coach to get hired by Clemson and N.C. State of the Atlantic Coast Conference. But his favorite project was Pete, who inherited his dad's passion for the sport. From the time his son was nine, Press worked diligently to develop Pete's ball-handling and shooting skills. The kid became so skilled at a young age that he would sometimes do halftime shows in which he would show off his magic with a ball.

Although Pete wanted to follow his idol Jerry West to West Virginia, he followed his dad when Press took the LSU job in 1966 for $15,000 per year. In those days, freshmen were ineligible for varsity competition, so Pete played for the freshman squad, creating an embarrassing situation. Many students would come for the freshman game to see Pete, then leave before the varsity game.

I was covering UK that winter, and I remember having dinner with Coach Rupp, his assistants, and a few fellow media types the night before the game. About halfway through the meal, Press Maravich showed up to pay his respects. As I recall it, he tried to tell Rupp about his kid, but Rupp was more interested in his bourbon and a sparkling blue vest that the restaurant owner had given him.

Over the next three varsity seasons (1967–70), LSU never beat Rupp's team. But the scoring battles between Maravich and UK's Dan Issel became one of the best shows in college basketball. Pete's dad gave him the green light to shoot at any time, from anywhere, and Pete responded by averaging almost forty-five points for his career, one of his many NCAA scoring records that will never be broken. And he did it without the benefit of the three-point shot, which wasn't introduced to college hoops until 1987.

With floppy hair, an orphan's face straight out of Dickens, and the trademark gray socks that drooped over his black Converse lowcuts, here he came, looking to make an acrobatic shot, a no-look, behind-the-back pass, or some other jaw-dropping play. He played to standing-room-only crowds for three seasons and spawned thousands of playground imitators.

Sadly, Pete never played in the NCAA tournament because, in those days, the tournament field was limited only to league champions and independents, and his teams just weren't good enough to qualify. However, his senior team was good enough to earn a berth to the NIT in Madison Square Garden, and *SI* assigned me to cover Mr. Show Biz in his debut in the world's entertainment capital.

To be frank, Pete wasn't at his best, and LSU was eliminated by the eventual NIT champs, Al McGuire's 1970 Marquette team, in the quarterfinals. However, *SI* still wanted me to do the piece, and the editors wanted a photo of Pete sitting in one of those horse-drawn carriages that take tourists through Central Park. They even wanted him to wear one of the top hats the drivers favored.

I went to Pete's hotel across from the Garden, and Bud Johnson, then LSU's sports information director, took me up to his room. We sat around, killing time until it was time to meet the *SI* photographer, when Bud suddenly keeled over and began having an epileptic seizure. Pete and I looked at each other in shock, and before I could say a word, he said, "You try to get your fingers down his throat to keep him from choking, and I'll go get my dad."

And then he was gone.

I tried to get Bud's mouth open, but his jaws were closed like a vise. I was starting to panic when here came Pete with Press in tow. Fortunately, Press knew what do to, and soon enough, Bud was back to normal, and we were on our way to Central Park.

After the photo shoot, Pete and I went into the bar at the Plaza Hotel to have a couple of drinks and review what had happened in the hotel.

"You S.O.B.," I said. "You didn't care about me getting my typing fingers bitten off."

"Man, I've got to take care of my hands," he said, laughing. "I'm getting ready to make a lot of money."

I never saw him again, except on television during his NBA career. I knew that in his later years, he found God and the peace he never had as a player. He died far too young, but he left a legacy that is worth remembering and celebrating. He was, after all, the first white man ever offered a contract to play *with* the Harlem Globetrotters.

I never thought Press Maravich was as dominating or driven as Arnold Spitz, the father of Olympic swimming icon Mark Spitz. When I was assigned to do a story on Mark in 1970, I ended up writing more about his dad than him because Arnold was far more interesting than Mark, a one-dimensional kid who was at a loss when asked to discuss anything except swimming.

Here was vintage Arnold:

"Because I've given of myself, this is what I created. He's a gorgeous human being, he's a beautiful person, it's terrible. You think this just happened? I've got my life tied up in this kid. You think I created a monster? He's beautiful, he's exceptional. There is nothing wrong with parents giving to their children. If people don't like it, the hell with 'em."

In maybe the best decision he ever made, Mark left California and his dad to swim for "Doc" Counsilman at Indiana. Of all the coaches I've ever met, in any sport, Doc was one of best motivators and students of people. During his IU career, Mark's self-esteem improved dramatically, setting him up perfectly to win a record seven gold medals at the 1972 Olympics in Munich.

I thought about Arnold Spitz when I met Earl Woods, the father of Tiger, during the 1996 NCAA golf championships at the Honors Course in Chattanooga. One lazy afternoon, Earl and I sat under an old shade tree behind the clubhouse, sipping iced tea and watching Tiger's lead grow on the scoreboard. Here are a few random quotes:

"I told him when he was a little boy that I would make two contributions: I would teach him mental toughness and course management."

"When Tiger was 10 years old, he told me he wanted a quality education. He said, 'I want to major in business and accounting so I can manage the people who manage my money.'"

"I gave him all the space he needs to develop and become the kind of person he wants to be. Love is a given; respect is earned. We've earned each other's respect. That's the way he'll treat others."

"Politics, in golf or business, has never entered our conversation. It's not that important to the success of an individual if you don't have goodness within."

"As a parent, you can only hope and pray and provide counseling and support. Your hands are limited. That's just the very nature of things. Fortunately for me, my son is not in love with material things. He's very laid-back and comfortable in his shoes."

Earl was a military officer who met Tiger's mother in Vietnam. He was a Christian, she a Buddhist. During Tiger's childhood, his dad worked with him every bit as much as Pete Maravich's dad did with him.

Before Earl's death in the summer of 2006, Tiger had won ten major championships and seemed a lock to break Jack Nicklaus' record of eighteen. He won four more in the next two years, but has not added to his fourteen total since 2008.

Without Earl around to guide him, Tiger went off the rails. He let his money and celebrity lead him to a series of sexual affairs that cost him his marriage and the brand that Earl had worked so diligently to build. He also has suffered a series of injuries that may be largely attributable to the strain his powerful swing put on his body.

But in August of 2018, at 42, Tiger rolled back the clock in the PGA Championship in St. Louis and finished second, only two shots behind winner Brooks Koepka. Maybe redemption still is in his future.

Archie Manning, my all-time favorite college football player, took a different route with his sons.

An outstanding all-around athlete from tiny Drew, Mississippi, Archie accepted a scholarship to play football at Ole Miss in the spring of 1966. That was only four years after the campus in Oxford had become a battleground over the enrollment of James Meredith, the university's first African American student.

In the spring of 1969, his father committed suicide, leaving Archie to care for his mother and sister. The tragedy made Archie grow up quickly. But it didn't keep him from becoming a southern folk hero in the 1969 season.

His unique name and Huck Finn looks had something to do with it. Mostly, though, it was because of his style, a combination of running and passing with a flair for the dramatic. He became more than a regional star as a junior, when his play in a nationally televised 33-32 loss to Alabama captivated fans everywhere.

I became so intrigued by Archie that, with the backing of Dan Jenkins, I talked the magazine into putting him on the cover of the 1970 college football issue. By the time I got to Oxford, his Heisman Trophy campaign was well under way. It didn't hurt that his girlfriend, Olivia Williams of Philadelphia, Mississippi, was a campus beauty queen. She was as mature as Archie and helped manage the hysteria.

Managing editor Andre Laguerre didn't want me to rehash Mississippi's racial strife, so I stuck strictly to football and the phenomenon of "Archie Fever." Although I didn't realize it until much later, it was the most positive national publicity the state had received in many years.

A broken left arm ruined Archie's Heisman chances, but it didn't keep interim coach Frank "Bruiser" Kinard from bringing him back for the big game against LSU. I met Archie in his motel room before the game, and he let me feel the metal plate holding his left radius together. However, with his arm encased in padding, Archie wasn't himself, and the Tigers won the game.

Archie and I stayed in touch during his ill-fated career with the hapless New Orleans Saints, and I was aware that he and Olivia had given birth to three sons — Peyton, Cooper, and Eli. Archie didn't push any of them into football, but they all ended up playing.

Archie has told me that Cooper might have been the most talented of the three, but he was forced to give up the game in college because of spinal stenosis. If that's the case, he must have been some kind of player because Peyton and Eli both quarterbacked their NFL teams to Super Bowl championships.

As I've watched Peyton and Eli, I can't help but feel badly that Archie's dad didn't live to see what his son and grandsons have done with their lives.

Over the years, it seems that the big money now available in sports has given us a new breed of parent. Exhibit A, of course, is LaVar Ball, the loutish father of three sons — Lonzo, LiAngelo, and LeMelo — whom he seemed to start marketing before they were all potty-trained.

He had their lives all planned out. All three would be one-and-done college players and members of the Los Angeles Lakers. He was so sure of their success that he even rolled out a brand of sneakers, Big Baller Brand, to make money off his sons.

He had to go to Plan B when LiAngelo and two of his UCLA team-mates were arrested for shoplifting on a trip to China. They were released after Donald Trump intervened on their behalf. But doggone if Trump and LaVar didn't get into a Twitter fight when the father refused to thank and praise Trump. The upshot was that LiAngelo got kicked off the team at UCLA and signed with a team in Lithuania, dragging his younger brother LeMelo with him.

Somehow, I can't see this story having a happy ending.

Chapter Eighteen

WAR (NOT REALLY) STORIES

In my day, every boy who turned eighteen could count on receiving a letter from the Selective Service Administration that began "Greetings." It was a notice that you were required by law to register for service in the U.S. Army. If you did not volunteer, you could be drafted at the Army's discretion.

I never worried much about the draft because I was told repeatedly that my poor eyesight would grant me a 4-F, or unfit for duty, classification. That was the case until the casualties in the Vietnam War grew so high that the military relaxed its standards in order to meet its quota of manpower.

For Muhammad Ali, who had initially been rejected because he had flunked an aptitude test, that decision led to the moment in Houston when he refused to step forward and join the Army on the grounds that he was a Muslim minister.

For me, it meant a visit to my good friend J.B. Faulconer, who then was second in command of Kentucky's 100th Division, U.S. Army Reserves. He said he had a spot for me in his public information office, so I quickly joined the 100th and was sent off to Basic Training at Fort Ord, California, in mid-May of 1967.

Nobody could ever explain to me why I was sent all the way to Fort Ord when Fort Knox was only twenty miles from my home. I once brought that up to an officer, and he only said, "Reed, you have a bad attitude." I guess I did, at least by Army standards.

The day I reported for duty at Fort Ord, I offered a suggestion about floor-buffing to PFC Teague, our assistant drill instructor. I'll never forget the evil smile on his face as he said, "Well, lookee here. . . . We have ourselves a collitch boy. . . . Collitch boy, drop and give me twenty pushups."

I didn't make another suggestion until I had completed my military and physical training, which enabled me to move on to clerk-typist school. I approached the officer in charge and said, "Sir, I can already type eighty-five words a minute. Do you think it would be possible for me to not take the typing classes?"

Well, of course, it wasn't. So, I took all the typing classes. On our final exam, it was determined that — you guessed it — I could type eighty-five words a minute. I think I still have the plaque they gave me for being the school's honor graduate.

After moving to New York in the summer of 1968, the Army assigned me to a small public information unit that met monthly in an old armory on 42nd Street, between Ninth and Tenth Avenues. The unit was commanded by Col. Wilford Horne, a career civil servant for the City of New York. He was assisted by Warrant Officer Vincent Vastola, also a lifelong public servant who had about him a frazzled, confused, perpetually perplexed manner.

Their troops mostly were members of the New York media or advertising business, a lot of sharp guys who took great delight in goofing off and making the officers' lives miserable. Naturally, I fit right in.

At one time or another, our unit included Marv Albert, the voice of the New York Knicks; Bud Harrelson, the shortstop of the New York Mets; and well-known radio news anchors Bob Hardt, Tim O'Donnell, and Ernie Asnastos. Our top sergeant — Col. Horne always called him "Top" in true military fashion — was Bob Dilenschneider, an upcoming advertising executive who eventually founded his own successful firm.

But the two guys I found the most intriguing were David Kennerly and Stanley G. Mortimer III.

Kennerly was a brash young guy who worked as a photographer for United Press International. As soon as he heard I worked for *Sports Illustrated*, he quizzed me about getting a job there. He liked to drop the names of famous people he had photographed, which I took with a grain of salt until the day three of us had gotten excused from the armory on some pretext and were riding around Manhattan, killing time.

"Hey, there's Mia," Kennerly said.

While he rolled down his window, the two of us looked over, and, sure enough, there was the actress Mia Farrow, star of *Rosemary's Baby*, standing on a corner, waiting for a light to change.

"Mia!" shouted Kennerly. "Hey, Mia!"

I slid down in my seat, embarrassed that Kennerly was making a fool of himself. But doggone if Ms. Farrow didn't look over and wave, saying "Dave . . . how are you, Dave?"

After his Reserve days were up, Kennerly talked the UPI into sending him to Vietnam, where one of his photographs earned him a Pulitzer Prize. Soon thereafter, he became the personal photographer to President Gerald Ford.

During Ford's campaign against Jimmy Carter in 1976, he made a brief stop in Louisville on Air Force One. Kennerly had contacted me, and we made arrangements to meet for a drink while the President was giving his speech. I was grateful he had the good grace to not mention the time I pretty much ignored him when he asked about working for *SI*.

As for Stanley G. Mortimer III, he was a tall, quiet fellow who had "patrician" written all over him. One of the guys in the unit discovered that Stanley's father was an heir to the Standard Oil fortune and that his mother was "Babe" Paley, the famed New York socialite and wife of William S. Paley, the founder and head of CBS.

One day, during another excused outing from the armory, Stanley took me to his family home on the north shore of Long Island. It was like walking into the set of *The Great Gatsby*. I didn't know until then that some people really lived like that.

But Stanley never talked about his wealth or acted snobby. He wanted to be just one of the guys, and we were happy to accommodate him. At one summer camp in Indiantown Gap Military Reservation near Hershey, Pennsylvania, he and I roomed together in a barracks. He taught me how to find cheap wines that were almost as good as the expensive ones.

I'll always remember the day that Col. Horne called Stanley into his office at the armory. He left the door open and I was right outside, sweeping the floor, so I got to overhear their conversation.

"Mortimer," said Col. Horne, sternly, "you missed the last meeting."

"Yes, sir, I did," said Stanley.

"You know what that means, don't you?"

"No, sir," said Stanley. "What?"

"I'm going to have to dock you in pay."

"Gee, sir," said Stanley. "I guess I'll have to make it up somewhere else."

Outside the office, I had to drop the broom and go somewhere to laugh. No, make that howl. It was, and still is, one of the funniest things I've ever head — and Stanley pulled it off with a straight face.

Another time, Col. Horne and Mr. Vastola decided they needed to shape us up by taking us on an overnight bivouac at Fort Totten near Brooklyn. We decided to show them what we thought about that. So, at dinner time, while they were opening their little tins of Army-issued rations, the troops produced a red-and-white checked tablecloth, candles, bottles of wine, and pasta. I still don't know how we escaped court martial.

In the winter of 1971, the U.S. Postal workers went on strike in New York City, and President Richard Nixon declared a state of national emergency and activated the Reserves and National Guard to deliver the mail.

I canceled a trip and reported to the armory to get my orders. I was assigned to go to a little room at JFK Airport and sit by a phone. If the phone rang, I was supposed to answer it. That's all I was told.

For three days, I sat by that phone. It never rang. And then the strike was resolved, and we were deactivated to resume our normal lives. A few weeks later, I was with Bud Harrelson and a few other guys when we got the news that the fine print in the Reserve contract had a clause that said if a Reservist was ever called up for active duty, he got a year cut off his six-year commitment.

It was one of the great moments of my life.

I didn't hate the Army, but I did hate the Vietnam War. It was so different from World War II, when America was literally fighting for its survival. The entire nation was invested in that war, and many famed baseball players — Ted Williams, Bob Feller, Hank Greenberg, and many more — gave up prime years on the diamond to join one of the services.

Joe Louis, the world heavyweight boxing champion, joined the Army and was assigned to entertain the troops by fight exhibitions. That probably would have been Muhammad Ali's lot had he joined the Army, although his adoption of the Muslim religion changed the way many Americans thought about him. While Louis was considered a "good black" who knew his place, Ali was a defiant radical.

I was very close to enlisting during the Cuban Missile Crisis of 1962. The Russians had set up missiles with atomic warheads only miles from our mainland, a threat that was easy to understand. But Vietnam was different. Nobody knew where it was or why we were sending so many troops there. When it was revealed that our government had been lying to us about body counts and other matters, it killed any idealism or patriotism that any of us had remaining.

Today I sometimes go to games where military veterans are asked to stand up, so the crowd can applaud them. I've stood up a couple of times — I do have an honorable discharge from the Army — but usually I don't because the applause should go to the real heroes, the troops who served in combat, instead of a non-entity like me.

I've often thought about the guys with whom I went through basic training at Fort Ord. Our company consisted of enlistees, draftees, reservists and National Guardsmen. After our training, the reservists and guardsmen got to go home, but many of the enlistees and draftees were sent directly to Vietnam.

I hope God has blessed them all.

Chapter Nineteen

THE GENERAL

Of all the famous and accomplished people I've been fortunate to know and cover, one draws about three times as many questions as the rest of them combined. Love him or hate him, and there are no shades of gray, the public is fascinated by Bob Knight, who coached basketball with great distinction — and as much controversy — at Indiana University from 1972 through 2000.

The questions I've gotten about Knight — and still do — run the gamut from "What's he really like?" to "How can you defend that jerk?" I've sometimes asked myself the same questions, and it became more difficult as the years went on. The game of basketball changed, and society changed, but Bob never did.

I must admit right off that we used each other. I knew it, and so did he. I got access to the biggest newsmaker in the *Courier-Journal's* circulation area. He got the benefit of the doubt from the sports editor of a newspaper that was known nationwide for the quality of its college basketball coverage. In retrospect, I'd say it was a "push," the gambling term for a tie.

But there was more, too. Growing up in Orrsville, Ohio, Bob listened to George Walsh call the University of Kentucky games on 50,000-watt WHAS radio, the Bingham-owned station in Louisville. He was fascinated by Rupp, and he loved to pick my brain about what it was like to cover him. I can still get a laugh out of Bob with my imitation of Rupp's Kansas twang.

I also think Bob picked up on my genuine love of college basketball and desire to learn everything about it I could. So, by letting me see his program from the inside out, he knew I would get an understanding of his methods that nobody except Bob Hammel of the *Bloomington News-Telegraph*, and maybe a couple of others, was allowed to have.

An IU faculty member once told me that Bob was the best teacher on campus, and I believe that. His players were required to keep notebooks. Before almost every practice, he would tell them things to put in their notebooks. Then they would go out on the floor and put the notes into practice. Then they would come back into the locker room and get more instruction.

He was strict about the importance of academics and compliance with the NCAA rules, and far as I was concerned, that made it much easier to defend him. He represented so much that was good about college basketball, but he also gave his detractors plenty of ammunition to berate him — the chair-throwing, the arrest in Puerto Rico when he was coaching the U.S. Pan-American team, the comments to NBC's Connie Chung that when rape was inevitable, you "might as well enjoy it." (He claimed she agreed to edit that out, only to double-cross him.)

But the fans in Indiana loved him. Lord, did they ever! One night I went to a booster club meeting with him somewhere in southern Indiana. He took off on the media, as he was wont to do from time to time, and finally pointed a finger at me, "There's one of them!" he said. The fans booed me lustily. Later, he laughed and said, "You know that if I told them to string you up, they would have done it, don't you?" And then I laughed along with him, although mine was a bit strained.

During the aforementioned Pan-Am Games, a player from Cuba hit the Americans' Kyle Macy of Kentucky in the jaw and broke it, forcing Macy to come home early. When Knight got back, he called and told me he was coming to Lexington to personally present Macy with his gold medal. The only media there were me and a photographer.

In 1984, after Knight's U.S. team had won the gold medal in the Los Angeles Olympic Games, Knight allowed Hammel and I to be the only U.S. writers to get into the locker room. I distinctly remember young Michael Jordan, who was going to skip his senior season at North Carolina to go into the NBA draft, smoking a cigar.

Knight spent most of his time talking with Henry Iba, the iconic Oklahoma State coach who was one of Knight's coaching idols. Earlier, Knight had told his victorious players to carry Iba off the floor, not him, so the old man could get the victory ride he missed in 1972, when international basketball officials literally stole the gold from Iba's U.S. team and gave it to the Soviet Union.

But the story that best explains the kind of relationship I had with Bob began in the fall of 1985, when I learned that John Feinstein, a talented young writer at the *Washington Post*, whom I had met through

Dave Kindred, had been given a leave of absence, so he could spend the entire 1985–'86 season in Bloomington. As it was told to me, Knight had agreed to give him almost total access.

I had lunch with John at Hasenour's on his way to Bloomington. He was a Duke graduate, and he told me the way he had gotten the book deal was that Coach Mike Krzyzewski had told Knight he could trust John to be honorable. But since John had a fairly healthy ego of his own, I was skeptical. I called Kindred and said, "If they make it to the new year, I'll be shocked."

Well, sure enough, the winter was filled with stories about Knight and John getting on each other's nerves, to put it kindly. But they got through the season, and everybody in the basketball world looked forward to the book's release just before the 1986–87 season. Unsurprisingly, Knight hated it. He said he had made John promise to not quote his cursing because he didn't want his mother to read it; John said no such agreement had been made. And so forth.

One night when Bob's team was on the road, John had a huge book signing scheduled at an Indianapolis book store. Only a couple of hours before the IU game, Knight called me from the Indiana locker room and asked me to go to the book signing and act as a sort of one-man "truth squad" on his behalf. I told him I couldn't do it because I probably would have gotten fired. He angrily slammed down the phone, and we never discussed it again.

After the book's release, I got a lot of questions from readers wanting to know what I thought about it. I decided the column should run the Tuesday before the UK-Indiana game in Bloomington. But Gannett had replaced my friend Slusher with a guy who didn't like me, and he tried to assign me to something else rather than run the column about *Season on the Brink.*

That was my first clue that Gannett intended to make me so unhappy that I would leave. I did exactly that a few days later, when I was told that my only choice was to return to the sports department under probation for "insubordination" and do as I was told. When my attorney J. Bruce Miller heard that, he said, "This party's over," and it was. On the way out of the building, Bruce said, "That wasn't a meeting; it was an assassination."

With the help of Jim Host, I started my own company with clients such as the *Herald-Leader*, WHAS radio and TV, WKYT in Lexington, the University of Louisville Equine Industry program, and Host Communications. Entrepreneurship was a little scary for a guy who always had worked for a paycheck, but it worked out rather well right from the start.

True to his word, Knight gave me permission to ghost-write a column that would run throughout the 1987 NCAA tournament. We worked out a deadline schedule, and with the assistance of Jim Host, who was helping me set up my own company, we lined up almost forty papers that agreed to buy it. The column would be distributed by the Associated Press.

As fate would have it, doggone if Knight and the Hoosiers didn't win the NCAA championship, beating Syracuse in the New Orleans Superdome on a buzzer-beating, leaning jump shot by Keith Smart. I'd say the papers who bought our column got their money's worth. Bob and I split the money, which wasn't a lot, but it was the gesture on his part that mattered most to me.

A few weeks after the season, he asked me to come to Bloomington and serve as master of ceremonies at the championship team's victory dinner in Assembly Hall. He didn't have to do that. He didn't have to agree to let me ghost-write his NCAA column. But he did because he's a stand-up guy, and I will be eternally grateful.

Bob's last great team at IU was the Calbert Cheaney bunch in 1992–93 that I really thought was going to win him his fourth NCAA title. But the Hoosiers couldn't overcome the loss of 6-9 Alan Henderson and were eliminated by Kansas in the NCAA Midwest Regional in St. Louis.

From that time on, I thought Bob grew increasingly sour on the game he loved. Even though he won the title in 1986–87, he hated the new rules that went into effect that year — three points for a jump shot past a 19'9" semi-circle and a shot clock to speed up play. Bob's idea was that you run your motion offense over and again until you get a bucket near the goal or a short jumper. He was all about picks, ball-handling, patience, and crisp passing. But all that was devalued by the new rules, in his mind.

The mid-1990s also was the era when network TV money, shoe-company money, and AAU summer-camp money began to dominate and pervert the game. To Knight, they all were a bunch of predators who had no business in college basketball. He saw more coaches cheating and devaluing academics. Stubbornly, and admirably, he stuck to his ways rather than compromise his principles. But suddenly the best athletes were finding easier, softer places where the demands on them weren't exacting and everyone was lined up to kiss their butts.

For most of his career at IU, Bob was supported — some might say "enabled" — by President John Ryan and Athletics Director Ralph Floyd, who pretty much let him do things his way, even when his way brought embarrassment to the university. But just as the world changed for me when Gannett bought the *C-J*, so did it change for Bob when Myles Brand became the President of IU.

At times it seemed as if Brand's primary mission was to bring Knight under control. Perhaps he saw IU as mostly a means to an end, the end being President of the NCAA. Whatever, for the first time at IU, the president didn't have Knight's back. In fact, he applied so much pressure that he eventually got Bob to agree to a "zero tolerance" behavioral policy. Both sides had to know that Bob couldn't live up to it and still be Bob.

The final straw was a silly one. As Bob was walking back into Assembly Hall after practice, a student addressed him as "Hey, Knight." To the coach, it was an act of disrespect, and he told the student as much in his own special way. That was it for Brand. He fired Knight and, sure enough, was subsequently rewarded with the NCAA president's job.

During that time, Knight invited seven writers to come to Bloomington and ask him anything we wanted, no restrictions. This group, which Finestein called "The Silly Seven," included Bob Hammel and me, Dave Kindred of the *Atlanta Journal-Constitution* (he had moved from the *Washington Post*), Hubert Mizell of the *St. Petersburg Times*, Dick Fenlon of the *Columbus Dispatch*, and two others I can't recall, but they were from the *New York Times* and the *Chicago Tribune*.

Knight admitted that he never should have agreed to the zero tolerance policy. He had explanations for everything from grabbing player Neil Reed by the throat in a practice session that was caught on tape to firing assistant Ron Felling. But it didn't matter. His last act at IU was to attend a huge bonfire rally organized by students who protested his firing.

At Texas Tech, Bob found the same sort of supportive athletics director that he had enjoyed all those years at IU. He and his wife Karen, a native of Oklahoma, loved living in Texas. Although Lubbock, the home of Buddy Holly, is one of the toughest places in the world upon which to sell recruits, Bob built a couple of good teams down there and became the first coach to surpass 900 career wins. But one day, near the end of the 2008–09 season, he shocked everyone by just walking away. He and the game had just had enough of each other.

Bob's career as a TV analyst didn't last too long. He was very good when he was engaged, but he often seemed bored by the game as it's played today. I think he also felt it was beneath him to act interested in mediocre coaches who were making far more money than he ever made. Last time I heard, Bob and Karen were living out west, and he was indulging his passion for hunting and fishing. I hope he's happy and at peace with himself.

Bob adopted a sort of scorched-earth policy when he left IU. He turned down all invitations to come back for reunions or simply to let the Hoosier fans cheer him one more time. I told him I wished he would change his mind, but he said, "Billy, I can't be the me that you want me to be — I have to be the me that I want me to be."

Chapter Twenty

MY FAB FINAL FOUR RUN

Because the *Courier-Journal* covered the Final Four long before most newspapers, the NCAA showed its appreciation by always giving the *C-J* sports editor a seat near midcourt on the front row of the press table, no matter who was playing. I got to take advantage of that special relationship from 1978–86, which gave me an excellent view of some classic games that are still being discussed, such as the 1979 matchup between Larry Bird of Indiana State and Earvin "Magic" Johnson of Michigan State, still the king of the championship game TV rankings.

In 1982, the NCAA put the Final Four in a domed stadium for the first time in order to accommodate the growing demand for tickets. It was surreal to stand on the floor in the Louisiana Superdome and gaze around at all those seats. It certainly didn't have the feel of a basketball arena and it still doesn't, yet the NCAA went to domes for good in 1997.

My first Final Four was also the first one for North Carolina coach Dean Smith. It came in 1967 at Louisville's Freedom Hall, the fifth of the six Final Fours held in that building between 1958 and 1969. I was assigned to cover Smith's Tar Heels when they arrived at Louisville International Airport (then Standiford Field), and doggone if they didn't get off the plane waving little Confederate flags.

In those days, that was considered to be only a showing of regional pride. The Tar Heels, after all, were the team from Dixie in a Final Four that also included Houston, UCLA, and Dayton. But can you imagine the furor that would cause today? Smith, a political liberal who became known for his strong stances in favor of integration, would have been fired on the spot and vilified as a racist. It's an interesting study in how perceptions change over time.

I was assigned to do the game story on North Carolina-Dayton (the Flyers upset the Heels behind hot-shooting forward Don May) and a sidebar on the highly anticipated showdown between 7-foot-1 Lew Alcindor's unbeaten sophomore team at UCLA and a talented Houston bunch led by Elvin "The Big E" Hayes and coached by Guy V. Lewis. Before the game, Hayes had predicted that Houston would upset the Bruins.

Well, it didn't happen. Like everyone else in college basketball, Houston had no answer for Alcindor (later Kareem Abdul-Jabbar) and his supporting cast. After the game, thinking I would write about Hayes' reaction, I fell in behind the Big E as he walked off the floor and headed toward the locker room, which was closed to the press. However, since I was only twenty-three, I must have looked like a student manager because the guard didn't stop me as I followed Hayes into the small, steamy room.

That year the NCAA didn't have mandatory post-game press conferences the way it has done for years. But it did have a designated person in the locker room who conducted interviews that were piped by closed-circuit TV to another room where the writers had gathered. When somebody saw me in the background, talking to Hayes, a mighty roar of protest ensued.

What made it worse — or better, from my standpoint — was that Hayes gave me some great stuff. He accused his teammates of choking and said that Alcindor was over-rated. When the editors in the *C-J* office got my story, they immediately moved it to the front sports page and displayed it prominently. I guess you could say it was my first major "scoop."

The next night — the Final Four was played on Friday and Saturday nights in those days — the NCAA put out a news release apologizing to the media for the presence of an unauthorized writer in the Houston locker room. I tried to look and sound apologetic when I was reprimanded by the NCAA media staff, but I was smiling inside. I had gotten the story. That's all that really mattered to me.

That was the beginning of twenty-four Final Fours for me, and I enjoyed them all. Others have covered more, but I don't think anybody has ever had a better run, in terms of being close to the champions, than I had from 1975–87. See if you agree.

1975 — Both UK and U of L made the Final Four in San Diego, but U of L's overtime loss to UCLA in the semifinals kept them from meeting for the title, which was decided when John Wooden's last UCLA team defeated UK. Almost all the writers were sure that Denny Crum would leave U of L to replace Wooden, but he stayed put and the job went to Gene Bartow of Memphis State.

1976 — I missed the Final Four in Philadelphia and the completion of Indiana's unbeaten season because I was doing the *C-J* general column and really had no good excuse to be there. But Indiana's championship led me to go to Bloomington and do a two-part series on Knight, the beginning of our friendship.

1977 — I covered the Mideast Regional in Rupp Arena for *Sports Illustrated,* which gave me the opportunity to hang around with North Carolina-Charlotte coach Lee Rose, who had been C.M. Newton's assistant when I was at Transylvania. Lee's top two assistants were Mike Pratt, who had played at UK with Dan Issel, and Everett Bass, one of his Transy players.

After Charlotte had defeated Michigan to go to the Final Four, *SI* got me some tickets in the stands, where I pulled for Lee to upset Al McGuire and Marquette in the semis. It looked like it was going to happen until a last-second bucket by Marquette's Jerome Whitehead put McGuire's last Marquette team into the championship game, where it defeated North Carolina.

1978 — UK ripped Duke in the title game behind Jack Givens' forty-one points to give Hall the NCAA title he needed to get the Adolph Rupp loyalists off his back. I remember flying home with the team and being met at around 4 a.m. by a huge crowd at Blue Grass Airport.

1979 — I covered the Midwest Regional in Cincinnati for both *SI* and the *C-J*, and my piece on Indiana State's last-second win over Arkansas made the *SI* cover. The winning basket wasn't scored by Bird but by Bob Heaton, whose follow-up shot spoiled a second straight Final Four trip for Coach Eddie Sutton's "Triplets" — Sidney Moncrief, Melvin Delph, and Ron Brewer.

Despite all the hoopla over Indiana State-Michigan State, it actually was only a so-so championship game. The star was neither Bird nor Magic but Greg Kelser, a Michigan State forward who was the beneficiary of some terrific passing by Johnson. When Magic left for the NBA after his sophomore season, his rivalry with Bird pumped new life into the pro league.

1980 — Louisville finally won its first championship with one of the most enjoyable teams I ever covered. The star, of course, was Darrell Griffith, whose high-flying antics earned him the nickname "Dr. Dunkenstein." The rest of the starting lineup included sophomore guard Jerry Eaves and three engaging freshman — effervescent forward Derek Smith, glowering center Rodney McCray, and cutup forward Wiley Brown, who made news before the title game against UCLA by losing his artificial thumb. (It was found in a Dumpster at the team hotel.)

1981 — About halfway through the season, IU Coach Bob Knight finally came to an understanding with Isiah Thomas, his brilliant point guard. Knight agreed to give Thomas more freedom, and Thomas agreed to play with more discipline. Maybe that's what caused the light bulb to come on for 6-foot-10 sophomore forward Landon Turner, and maybe it wasn't, but Thomas and Turner turned the Hoosiers into a team of beauty that won Knight his second title in Philadelphia on the night that President Ronald Reagan was wounded there by a would-be assassin.

1982 — The beginning of the Dome era also was the ending of Dean Smith's quest for the national title. Although 7-foot-2 Georgetown freshman Patrick Ewing owned the paint, a jump shot from the side by North Carolina freshman Michael Jordan and a subsequent turnover by Georgetown's Freddie Brown sealed the deal for the Heels. To gain the finals, Georgetown had defeated U of L in the semis.

1983 – After its historic win over UK in Knoxville, U of L faced Houston's ballyhooed "Phi Slamma Jamma" team in the high altitude of Albuquerque, New Mexico. This was supposed to be the real national championship game because both U of L and Houston seemed far better than North Carolina State and Georgia, the surprise competitors in the other semifinals. As advertised, the Cards and Coogs went dunk-to-dunk until Houston went on a 21-0 spree against the oxygen-deprived Cards. Inexplicably, Crum didn't call a timeout to interrupt the run and give his players a breather. That set up what is still the greatest upset in championship history, N.C. State beating Houston on a last-second follow shot by Lorenzo Charles.

1984 — The Final Four was held in Seattle's Kingdome, so it was only fitting the participating teams had such giant rulers as Georgetown's Ewing, Houston's Akeem Olajuwon, and Kentucky's Sam Bowie and Melvin Turpin. The Cougars easily made it to the championship game for the second consecutive year, but Georgetown trailed UK at halftime and seemed to be in trouble until the Wildcats suddenly couldn't shoot straight. In the second half, even with two 7-footers in the lineup, the Cats went 3-for-33 from the floor. Nobody was more baffled than UK coach Hall, who attributed the loss to "extra-terrestrial" forces. Once again, Houston found a way to lose the title game, making Georgetown's John Thompson the first African American coach to win the D-I championship.

1985 — For the first time since 1969, the Final Four came to Kentucky, but this time the site was Lexington's Rupp Arena instead of Louisville's Freedom Hall. The excitement over the four teams — Georgetown, Memphis State, St. John's, and Villanova — was overshadowed by speculation over who was going to replace Hall, who had resigned after losing to St. John's in tournament play.

Three of the teams — Georgetown, St. John's, and Villanova — came from the Big East Conference, a fairly new league formed by Dave Gavitt, the former coach at Providence. Georgetown and Villanova advanced to the finals, and the Hoyas were regarded as overwhelming favorites to win their second consecutive title. It was said, in fact, that it would take a perfect game to beat them, and that's exactly what Villanova delivered. Hitting 80 per cent of its shots from the floor and using 6-foot-9 Ed Pinckney to frustrate Ewing defensively, Coach Rollie Massamino's Wildcats from Philadelphia scored another one for underdogs everywhere.

1986 — The story line for the championship game was Duke's students against Louisville's athletes, the implication being that the Cardinal players didn't care much about their studies. U of L guard Milt Wagner didn't help matters much when he was asked if he knew anything about Drexel, the Cards' first-round opponent. "That's one of them academic schools, isn't it?" said Milt.

Much as I admired Duke, Coach Mike Krzyzewski, and the players, I resented seeing the Cardinals ridiculed because they didn't have any Phi Beta Kappa candidates on their roster. These were kids who, in many cases, came from the city streets and underprivileged backgrounds. Nevertheless, the media had a field day with the contrast.

The Cards won Crum his second title because Wagner, not Duke's Johnny Dawkins, was the best guard on the floor and because Duke couldn't shut down Pervis "Never Nervous" Ellison, the Cards' stoic 6-foot-10 freshman center. Afterward, when I asked Crum how he felt

With Rick Bozich of the Louisville Times *before the 1983 UK-U of L "Dream Game" in Knoxville, Tennessee.*

Attendees of the Bill King luncheon, back, l-r: Denny Crum, Jim Bolus, Dr. Rudy Ellis, Gene Sullivan, Paul Rogers, Paul Hornung, Jim Thornton, Bill Boone, Jim Crutcher, Bill Malone, and Billy. Front: Mike Barry, Pee Wee Reese, King, Kenny Smith, Randy Sheen.

Billy on the bench before a Milwaukee Bucks' exhibition at Rupp Arena, 1978.

On the bench during a Morehead State University basketball exhibition at Shelby County High, 1980.

Billy, Cowboy Steve Taylor, and Henry Clay High School (later Duke and Georgia) basketball player, Frank Harscher.

Billy with University of Louisville Assistant Coach Bill Olsen and Jerry Eaves after the 1980 National Championship.

Media game before Milwaukee Bucks exhibition in Rupp Arena, 1978.

Coach Rick Pitino and the 1996 University of Kentucky NCAA Basketball Champions.

Billy Reed with Coach Bobby Knight and a fan, July 1985. Photo by John Nation.

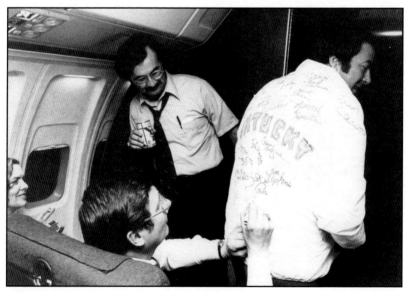

With Joe B. Hall on a plane home from St. Louis after the University of Kentucky's 1978 title.

Bob Knight with Billy, 1981.

SI cover after Seattle Slew won the Belmont Stakes to become the first unbeaten Triple Crown winner, 1977.

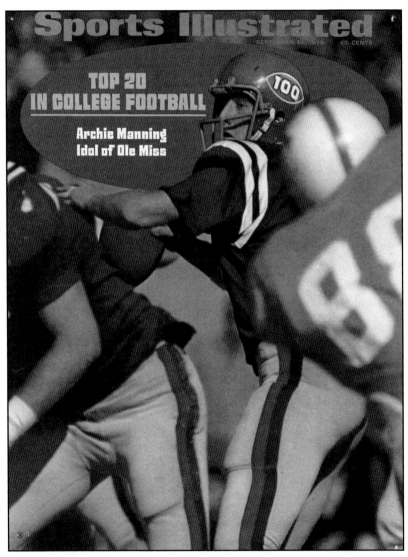

Billy's first SI *cover story, 1970.*

SI's Frank Deford did a cover story on Coach Rupp during the 1965-'66 season.

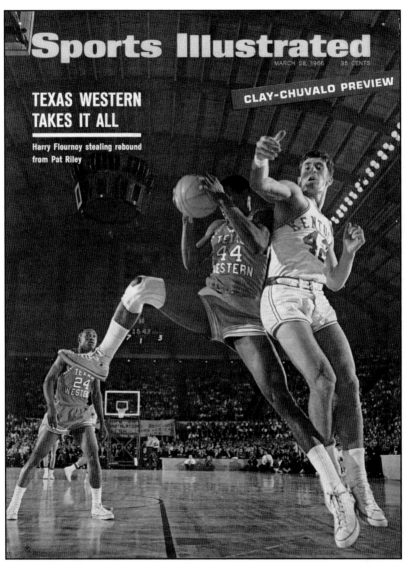

The game that became known as the "Brown versus Board of Education" of college basketball.

Call 'em off!

C̄ MAR 3 1 1976 E 7

Elvis fans take up their poison pens

All right, all right, I surrender. You Elvis Presley fans out there can put away your poison pens. You've taught me a lesson. If it's not nice to fool around with Mother Nature, it's suicide to take on The King.

Last week in this space, I wrote a column about Elvis and his weight problem. I meant it to be a humorous lament about what happens when all of us, even big-time sex symbols, grow old. Instead, you would have thought I had thrown a bomb at the Statue of Liberty.

One reader called me a "twerp," and that was one of the nicer comments. I thought about asking Barry Bingham Jr. for a bodyguard, except I don't think he has any to spare. Wonder if the Foreign Legion would consider taking a guy my age?

Nevertheless, I'm going to be fair about this. If I'm going to exercise my journalistic right to write what I want about Elvis, then I also ought to print what his fans think about me and my column. I'd like to print each letter in total, but, since there's room for only so much hate in one column, I've edited them down to the most sanguine comments.

Colleen Hunt, Shively: "I found your article on Mr. Presley disgusting . . . . I bet you are one of those insensitive people who point at afflicted people on the street and make unkind comments . . . . If the point of this letter wasn't only to comment on your 'writing,' I could mention your puffy face and the fact that you need a shave and you probably don't see as well as you did at 18 . . . ."

Dorothy Nichols, Gloria Houtchins, Janet Rose and Margaret Wick, Louisville: ". . . Actually it's none of any of our business how heavy or thin he is. It won't matter to us if he gains another 100 pounds. His voice is still as tremendous as it ever was and he

billy reed

Courier-Journal Columnist

A younger, sli[...] Elvis Presley, belted out a s[...] 1956. At far [...] he's still belting out in 1976, but t[...] a bit more of h[...] put i[...]

still has more looks and sex appeal in his little finger than anybody else . . . ."

Sue Kelly, Franklin, Ind.: " . . . Tell me, Mr. Reed, can you move like Elvis? I doubt it . . . . From the looks of your picture, you need Weight Watchers yourself. How would you like to be called a whale or Moby Reed? . . . . You mentioned his puffy face. Puffy and bloated is not the same as fat. Your face is F-A-T . . . Long live the King!"

Marita G. Griffin, New Albany: "You fuzzy-headed little twerp, when I first read that pathetic group of words you call a column, well, you can thank God that you were out of my reach. But now that I have calmed down and cooled off, I can look at it objectively and chalk the whole sorry mess up to ignorance and jealousy . . . . If Elvis weighed 500 pounds his true fans and lovers would be sitting in the audience screaming 'Roll him out' until he got there . . . . This column will line my garbage can, for that's where it belongs, although I would really

and truly like to shove it right down your throat."

Mrs. Fayola Turley, Lexington: ". . . . I think your opinion of one of the most fascinating and super stars of all time is strictly for the birds (the coo-coo's) . . . . I would like one day to meet you . . . . You appear to be as heavy if not heavier than Elvis."

Barbara Farmer, Lexington: " . . . Regardless of how much 'lard' there is, Mr. Presley still has the charisma it takes to be one of the world's top performers."

Sheila Sturgeon, Valley Station: . . . Elvis is the King of Music and will still be on top years from now!"

Sally G. Snyder, Louisville: ". . . I was so hurt with the words I read. I really wouldn't have expected such a review from you. Not even an enemy would I speak of the way you spoke of Elvis . . . . What does he have to do to win your approval as a fine entertainer as well as a man?"

Mrs. Darlene Lidster, Fairdale:

An Elvis column during Billy's tenure as the Courier–Journal's *general columnist (1974-'77).*

Cover of Louisville Magazine, *summer of 1985.*

Billy looks on as Coach Charlie McClendon of Louisiana State University (left) and Coach Bear Bryant of the University of Alabama greet each other midfield following the LSU-Alabama football game, November 1979. The Tide won 3-0.

Actor-comedians Foster Brooks and Bob Hope with Billy at the Foster Brooks Pro-Celebrity Golf Tournament, Louisville, 1986.

Preparing for a golf outing are Jim Dinwiddie and Frank Ham of the University of Kentucky, Billy, and Bill Malone.

Billy with Bob Hope (around 1986).

Golfing with Edgar Allen of Churchill Downs (back golf cart), Mike Battaglia and Paul Rogers.

Press tent at The Masters, Augusta, Georgia, 1986.

The bookends are all-time U of L basketball great Charlie Tyra (left) and Scooter McCray (right), a Cards' star in the 1980's.

Billy with Woody Fryman, pitcher for the Cincinnati Reds, at his farm in Flemingsburg, Kentucky. A left-hander, Woody was known as "The Fleming Flame."

Billy with Pee Wee Reese, shortstop of the Brooklyn Dodgers from 1941-'57. To his teammates, PeeWee was simply "The Captain."

With Governor Ernie Fletcher, who served from 2003-'07.

Frank Deford of Sports Illustrated *and Pee Wee Reese at a Cystic Fibrosis Dinner.*

Pee Wee Reese at Cystic Fibrosis Celebrity Waiter Dinner.

Billy enjoys a University of Louisville football game with Muhammad Ali, 2009.

Billy with quarterbacks Archie Manning, Peyton Manning and Johnny Unitas.

Transylvania University fraternity brothers, 2017. Pictured l-r: Bruce Davis, Bill Poulson, Larry Langan, Finbarr Saunders, Billy, and Glen Bagby.

Transylvania University fraternity brothers at Litchfield, South Carolina. Back, l-r: Billy, Larry Langan, Finbarr Saunders, and Bruce Davis. Front: Glen Bagby and Bill Poulson.

Billy with the Courier-Journal *private plane, which he often used in his days as the paper's general columnist (1974-'77).*

Billy on his 1977 tour for his book "Famous Kentuckians."

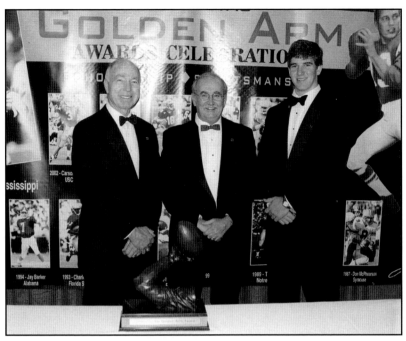

Bart Starr of the Green Bay Packers, Billy, and Eli Manning of Ole Miss University at a 1998 Johnny Unitas dinner.

Panel of Billy, Bill Nack of Sports Illustrated, Ed Schuyler of Associated Press, and Skip Bayless of ESPN at a horse racing seminar.

Photo of Billy Reed that ran with his general column in The Courier-Journal, *1974-77.*

Jim Bolus & Billy accepting the National Headliners Award from Miss America Terry Anne Mechwser at Atlantic City, 1973.

With Mr. William T. Young in the Keeneland paddock.

Billy with legendary Paul Hornung, former football icon at Louisville Plaget High, Notre Dame (1956 Heisman winner), and Vince Lombardi's Green Bay Packers.

Mike Pollio, Kenny Klein, Tom Jurich, and Billy tour Papa John's Cardinal Stadium before its completion in 1998.

Pictured l-r: Mike Barry, Dale Owens, Billy Reed, and Bill King, June 1980.

Interviewing University of Kentucky Quaterback Derrick Ramsey in 1977. Derrick would later become a good friend and colleague.

Billy with Transylvania University coaches Lee Rose, C.M. Newton, and Don Lane.

Billy Reed, July 1985. Photo by John Nation.

With A.B. "Happy" Chandler at Commonwealth Stadium.

Billy with Country music legend Loretta Lynn, circa 1976.

On hand to help Billy accept the Lexington Sports Commission's Tom Hammond Award were (L-R) grandaughter Caroline Frederick, daughter Amy Frederick, grandaughter Lucy Frederick (in front of me), daughter Susan Reed, sister Judy Reed, aunt Betty Reed, cousin Joellen Reed, and fraternity brother Bruce Davis (back right), 2017.

One-room school in Eastern Kentucky, Christmas 1975.

Billy's office at C-J when he was general columnist.

The Courier-Journal *building in Louisville.*

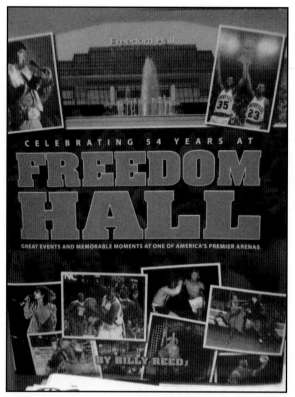

The cover of Billy's book "Celebrating 54 Years at Freedom Hall."

Ali pointing to his dad at a welcome home celebration after a win over Spinks in New Orleans.

Billy with Billy Hamilton of the Cincinnati Reds.

Billy with ACC Commissioner John Swofford.

Billy's plaque at the Kentucky Athletic Hall of Fame in Freedom Hall.

Billy (front row center) with the 1972 Olympic basketball team.

Billy and his daughters at the Derby.

Coach Adolph Rupp, being interviewed by Claude Sullivan.

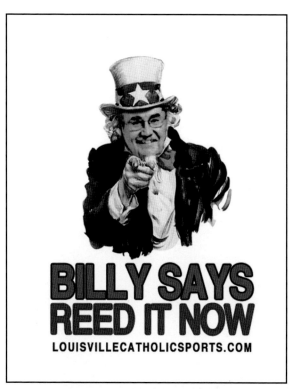

A promo for Louisville Catholic Sports.

Billy with Kenny Davis of the 1972 Olympic team and Georgetown College.

Billy and Lee Corso.

Billy and former coach Dale Brown of LSU.

Billy with former coach Bob Knight of Indiana and Texas Tech universities.

Front page of the Courier-Journal after University of Louisville's national title, 1980.

Billy and Lonnie Ali.

Billy with Super Bowl quarterback Phil Simms of the New York Giants.

A Freedom Hall press table in the early 1980s - Billy at far left.

Trainer Bob Baffert, his wife Jill, and Billy.

Billy with boxing legend Larry Holmes at an SI dinner honoring Muhammad Ali.

Billy and daughter Susan at Saratoga.

205

Billy with Darrell Griffith and Coach Denny Crum.

Pictured r-l: Dick Enberg, Billy and Tom Hammond of NBC.

Pictured r-l: Derrick Ramsey, his wife, Lee, Billy, and Billy's friend Leon Middleton.

Plaque at Georgetown College honoring Billy's "Conversations with Champions" series on KET.

Bill Malone and Billy at Paul Brown Stadium in Cincinnati.

Tom Callahan of Newsweek and Billy in back; Jim Bolus and Dave Kindred in front.

about the second title, he said, "The first one I felt mostly relief; this one puts you in a special category."

1987 — Although I was no longer with the *C-J*, I was writing for the *Herald-Leader* and ghost-writing a syndicated column for Bob Knight, so my friends at the NCAA made sure I had a good seat on the front row, to the left of the IU bench and looking down one of the baselines. It was from there that I saw Keith Smart rise into the air at the end of the title game against Syracuse and nail the jumper that gave Knight his third NCAA title. After the game, I walked with Knight and Bob Hammel from the Louisiana Superdome back to the team hotel. It was a nice way for my streak to end.

The 1988 season was the 50th anniversary of the Final Four, and the NCAA commissioned Host Communications to do a book about the event's history. Host asked me to provide the writers and Rick Clarkson, a friend from my *SI* days, to produce the photographs.

I did some of the writing myself, but I also begged and cajoled some of my friends to help out. So, in exchange for modest fees, I put together what I consider to be the greatest lineup of college basketball writers ever: Frank Deford, Dave Kindred, Michael Wilbon, Hubert Mizell, Bob Hammel, and others of their ilk. The book was on the plate of everyone who attended the NCAA's 50th anniversary banquet in Kansas City, and I was able to get a copy autographed by such immortals as Wooden, Jerry West, Tom Gola, Clyde Lovellette, and many more.

The 1996 Final Four, won by Coach Rick Pitino and Kentucky, was held at the Meadowlands in New Jersey, and it was the last held in a traditional arena. As I wandered around the floor in search of quotes, I couldn't help but remember the time twenty or so years earlier when Sonny Werblin had told me about his vision for a multi-sports complex on that very site.

Chapter Twenty-One

GOLF: A LOVELY
SORT OF TORTURE

I wish golf loved me as much as I love golf. I started playing in college and am still hacking today. At my, ah, best, I was a 22 handicap. But I've hit just enough good shots over the years to keep coming back, hoping my game can someday match the level of fun I have on the course with friends.

Fortunately for me, being able to play well is not a requirement for being able to write about it. I had to explain this to my friend Tom Musselman, a very good player, one year when I returned from covering the hallowed Masters in Augusta, Georgia.

"I read your stuff," Tom said, "and it was really good."

"Well, thanks," I said. "You seem surprised."

"I've seen you play," Tom replied. "I don't see how you can write about shots when you don't know what it's like to hit them."

"Tom." I laughed. "I've never ridden a Thoroughbred, either, but that doesn't stop me from covering the Kentucky Derby every year."

Of the four major classics, I've covered the Masters, U.S. Open, and PGA Championship multiple times. But I missed the British Open — "The Championship," as they call it — so that would be on my very short "bucket list" of events I'm sorry I missed.

I suppose the most significant golf "scoop" I ever got was when the Gahm family of Louisville let me have the story of their plans to build a "world-class" course on Shelbyville Road just east of Louisville. This was the course that was named Valhalla, and it became world-class, indeed, when it played host to the 2008 Ryder Cup. It also has been the site of the PGA championship three times and will be the scene of that event again in 2024.

For an area not nearly as well-known for its golf as its horse racing and basketball, Kentucky and Southern Indiana have produced a decent number of outstanding professional players, the most recent of whom may also prove to be the best — Justin Thomas, the Louisville St. Xavier grad who won the 2017 PGA Championship and enough other events to be named Golfer of the Year.

But the list begins with a female player, Marian Miley of Lexington, who was one of the nation's best amateur players in the 1930s. She and her mother lived at the Lexington Country Club, where her mother was in charge of the clubhouse, and both were murdered in their apartment in 1941. The story made national headlines, and finally a couple of workers at the club were arrested, tried, convicted, and executed.

In 1964, Bobby Nichols, another St. Xavier grad, won the PGA Championship, becoming the first Kentuckian to capture a major. Three years later, Gay Brewer Jr. of Lexington, who had played at Lafayette High and UK, won the Masters, still the only Kentuckian to earn the coveted green jacket that goes to the winner.

My love affair with the Masters did not get off to a happy start. The year was 1978, and because I was late putting in my credentials request, the only lodging available was in a private home instead of a motel. I got in late on Tuesday night and got up the next morning for a home-cooked breakfast, which was part of the deal.

The lady who owned the home sat with me and decided to test me on how I felt about African Americans. She made some racist comments that caused me to say, "Excuse me, but I can't stay here." So, I packed my bags and left, with no earthly idea of where to go. Fortunately, Dick Fenlon, my friend and counterpart with the *Louisville Times*, had an extra bed in his motel room, and he graciously let me use it for the rest of the week.

But my best Masters experience came the very next year. Fuzzy Zoeller of New Albany, Indiana, just across the Ohio River from Louisville, had qualified for his first Masters. I figured I'd follow him a couple of days to get the local angle, then begin covering the leaders after he missed the cut.

Well, much to the surprise of everyone, he not only made the cut, but he was also one of the leaders. And on Sunday, he won the green jacket in a playoff with Tommy Jacobs and Jack Nicklaus. His victory made me popular in the press tent with those writers who didn't know a thing about him and sought me out for information.

I also was there when Fuzzy won the 1984 U.S. Open at Winged Foot on Long Island, just outside New York City. Since the Open came only a week after the Belmont Stakes, I made plans to cover them both. The Belmont was won by Claiborne Farm's Swale, who also had won that year's Kentucky Derby, so I did a story and column on that and then, on Sunday, moved across the island to new quarters near the golf course.

But then came the news that Swale, while getting hosed down outside his barn on Sunday morning, had keeled over and died of an apparent heart attack. I called trainer Woody Stephens and Claiborne president Seth Hancock, who both were shaken by the loss. Only when that story was done was I able to begin concentrating on the U.S. Open.

It turned out to be a shootout between Fuzzy and his good friend Greg Norman, the blond Australian known as "The Great White Shark." On Saturday, when Norman hit an approach close to the pin on the 18th hole, Fuzzy walked on the green and waved a white towel at him. It was terrific golf theater that the public and the TV audience loved.

At about this time, maybe earlier, I met with Ed Mudd at the old Executive Inn across from the Kentucky State Fairgrounds. Ed was a teacher and coach who wanted to talk with me about his son, Jodie, who then was a star in the Commonwealth's amateur ranks. I decided he knew what he was talking about, so I jumped on the Jodie Mudd bandwagon.

The kid was supremely talented and nerveless. Nothing seem to rattle him. It was no surprise that he earned his PGA Tour card and began appearing on leaderboards around the nation. His game seemed especially suited for Augusta National, where he always played well, and I was totally convinced he would win the Masters, maybe more than once.

He reached the top in 1990, winning the PGA Tour Championship, known among golfers as the "fifth major." His future seemed unlimited. But then, shockingly, Jodie just walked away. He retired just as he was entering his prime. To this day, the only thing I can figure is that maybe he had just gotten burned out on golf. That sometimes happens to a prodigy, whatever his or her field of excellence.

I love golf at its highest levels because:

1. The players are independent contractors who have no guaranteed contracts. They start from scratch at the beginning of every year. They get what they earn.
2. Golfers are scrupulously honest, even calling penalties on themselves.

3. Golfers practice good sportsmanship and respect their opponents.

4. Golfers take accountability for their rounds, good or bad, and rarely make excuses.

5. Golfers generally are good with the public, which pays them back for respecting the game and its customs.

6. Golfers rarely get accused of sexual misconduct, using performance-enhancing drugs, or getting into bar fights.

Nevertheless, I have a problem with golfers. Probably because many of them come from privileged, country-club backgrounds, they don't have a well-defined social conscience. Unlike the Colin Kaepernicks of the sports world, they seem to live in a bubble where their most pressing concerns are the stock market and their endorsement contracts.

Like many others, I hoped that Tiger Woods would be the Jackie Robinson of his sport, a man of color determined to fight the sport's lily-white image and call for more clubs to open their memberships to minorities. But I gave up on that the time Tiger was playing in Chicago but refused to comment on a brutal killing that happened while the tournament was being played. I suppose he just didn't want to risk offending the people who bought his line of clothes and equipment.

The closest golfer to being a crusader for civil rights was Lee Trevino, the so-called "Merry Mex" from El Paso who became a national figure by winning the U.S. Open in 1969. Trevino was a driving-range hustler until he got a chance to play on the Tour. Inevitably, he did not exactly fall in love with Augusta National, where the only people of color wore either the white coveralls of a caddy or the formal attire of a clubhouse servant.

I got to meet Trevino four or five years ago, when Fuzzy Zoeller invited me to emcee the festivities at his final "Wolf Challenge" event at Covered Bridge, the semi-public course he owns near New Albany. His special guests were Trevino, Craig "The Walrus" Stadler, and Nancy Lopez, still possibly the best female player ever.

I had my picture taken with them, and trying to think about a clever caption, I recall what my golf buddy Mike Barry did after he and I had been photographed with Jack Nicklaus as Valhalla was under construction. (The Gahm family had hired Nicklaus to design the course.) Mike took a copy of the photo to Gene Sullivan, the pro at Wildwood, the club where we were members. The caption said, "Among them, these three golfers have won 18 major championships."

Speaking of Nicklaus, I was at Augusta in 1986, when he charged from off the pace to win the Masters. Everybody knew his best days were behind him, which made it all the more poignant as he walked up the 18th fairway on Sunday. What started as a murmur became a ground-shaking explosion of shouting and applause as the gallery rose to its feet to honor, one more time, the man who still remains the game's greatest player — and I mean that with all due respect to Ben Hogan, Sam Snead, Arnold Palmer, Tom Watson, Gary Player, Gene Sarazen, Trevino, Woods, and all of today's incredible young stars.

For several years in the late 1980s and early '90s, I was on the board of directors of the Foster Brooks Pro-Celebrity, an event held every Memorial Day at the Hurstbourne Country Club. Foster, of course, was the Louisville comedian whose main character, "The Lovable Lush," made him a big name in Las Vegas. He also was a regular on the network late-night and variety shows.

Although I got to meet a lot of pro golfers through the tournament, the celebrities intrigued me more. I got to share a few moments with the likes of former President Gerald Ford, show-business icon Bob Hope, and Victor Mature, the native Kentuckian who played Moses in *The Ten Commandments*.

But the one who gave me the biggest thrill was astronaut Neil Armstrong, the first man to walk on the moon. For one of the few times in my life, I literally was at a loss for words. He did not play heroes in movies or on TV; he was a real hero whose name and achievement will last as long as we have history books.

I never played in the Foster Brooks because my presence would have caused the event's liability insurance to skyrocket. However, I have played in a few Member-Guest tournaments, most recently the 2016 event at Hurstbourne. My host and partner played so well that we somehow made the shootout, where I even bogied the last hole we played.

That experienced only supported my belief that you don't have to play the game well to have a lot of fun on the course. Besides Mike Barry, I've played a lot over the years with people like Paul Rogers,

Lloyd "Pink" Gardner, my son-in-law Rob Frederick, Bill Poulson, Larry Langan, and Ron and Terry Sheeran. I can honestly say I have never had anything but a fun day while in their company.

I try to avoid golf snobs at all costs. You know the type because every club has them. They're sticklers for the most obscure of rules. The men wear long pants in 90-degree weather. They roll their eyes in disgust at a bad shot. They may shoot a lot of low numbers, but I think they miss the point of what makes the sport special.

The best golfer I ever played with was the late Larry Gilbert, who was an excellent club pro for many years before finally seeing if he could make it on the Senior Tour. Larry had arms like Popeye, the cartoon character, and could hit the ball a mile. We played together at some kind of Pro-Am in Lexington, and he couldn't have been more gracious, puffing on his trademark cigars and doing his best to put me at ease whenever I made a bad shot.

The cigars are what led to the lung cancer that killed Larry. I remember looking into his locker once at a Senior tournament and seeing stacks of cigar boxes sent to him by a manufacturer that wanted his endorsement. "Want a couple of boxes?" he said. "I can't smoke them all." He died less than a couple of years after winning the Senior Open in Detroit, a tournament I covered for *Sports Illustrated's* "Golf Plus" section.

I was shocked. The last time I talked with him, he sounded weak but wanted me to warn people against the dangers of smoking.

Chapter Twenty-Two

OLYMPICS TRIUMPH AND TRAGEDY

I think the greatest achievement in the sports world is to win an Olympics gold medal. I've covered two Summer Games, in 1968 for *Sports Illustrated* and in 1984 for the *Courier-Journal*, and both times they brought out the red, white and blue in me. I always get a little tingle when I see an American kid standing atop the victory stand, the gold around his or her neck, while our national anthem is played. If the athlete happens to be somebody I know, I even get a little teary-eyed.

It's not that I don't respect the athletes from other nations because I do. It's not that I'm some kind of xenophobe because I'm not. I respect other nations and their cultures. I believe that we must break down the artificial barriers that separate us. But still, there's just something about seeing one of our kids win that gold medal that gets to me unlike anything I've experienced in sports.

To tell the truth, the Olympics is why I left *SI* in 1972 and came back to Kentucky to rejoin the *Courier-Journal*.

I was a late addition to *SI's* 1968 Olympic team because the guy who was to be the reporter for lead writers John Underwood and Bob Ottum got fired for something or the other. The Olympics editor, Robert Creamer, picked me to replace him because I was more experienced than some my colleagues in the "bullpen" of Honor Fitzpatrick, the chief of reporters. So, I gave myself a crash course on the Olympic athletes, their sports, and home nations. I also learned that some kind of political struggle was going on in Mexico, which made me a bit nervous about going there.

The magazine rented a lavish home in the suburbs that was big enough to house two editors (Creamer and Roy Terrell), two senior writers (Underwood and Ottum), two reporters (Anita Verschoth and I), two photographers (Jerry Cooke and Rich Clarkson), and one house manager (Dita Comacheo). In addition, *SI* hired cars and local drivers to take us anywhere we wanted to go, which kept us from getting lost and out of the traffic jams. We ate most of our meals in the house.

Looking back, it was one of the most incredible experiences of my life. I was in the Olympic Stadium when Kip Keino of Kenya defeated Jim Ryun of Kansas in the 1,500-meters run, when John Carlos and Tommie Smith stood on the podium and raised black gloves to protest the Vietnam War, and when Bob Beamon shocked everyone by smashing the long-jump record.

Beamon's leap happened early in the day, during qualifying, and *SI* didn't have a photographer there to record it for posterity. Back in New York, managing editor Andre Laguerre was so upset that we almost could feel the earth tremble. Fortunately, we found a freelance photographer who had snapped the photo we needed, so a crisis was averted.

I visited a variety of the venues and learned something about weightlifting, gymnastics, and wrestling. I interviewed American swimming star Charlie Hickcox of Indiana and American swimming disappointment Mark Spitz of California. I was there when George Foreman won the gold in the heavyweight boxing division and when the U.S.A. continued its unbeaten streak in Olympic basketball. The star of the team was Spencer Hayward of Detroit, but my go-to guy for quotes was team captain Mike Silliman of the U.S. Military Academy, a native of Louisville who led St. Xavier High to the 1962 state championship before going off to West Point.

I must have done fairly well because, when we got back home, I began getting assignments to write about Olympians. I went to Santa Barbara, California, where I got to sit in a hot tub, despite cold weather, with decathlon champion Bill Toomey and his wife, the English sprinter Mary Rand. I did a follow-up piece on Hayward. Mostly, I became the magazine's swimming writer, which meant several trips to Bloomington, Indiana, to write about Hickcox, Spitz, and the dominating machine that Coach Doc Counsilman had put together.

In late December 1971, Olympics editor Gil Rogin called me into his office and told me I was going to be his swimming writer at the 1972 Games in Munich. It was totally unexpected because I had figured he might opt for an older writer. I was thrilled and not only because I had established a good relationship with Spitz, who had a shot at winning seven golds. I got home and told Alice that we were going to Germany the following summer.

For about six weeks, I was on a cloud. But then came the day when Rogin called me in again and said, "I'm really sorry, but the old man [Laguerre]overruled me and we're going to use Jerry Kershenbaum to cover swimming." To say I was crushed would be an understatement. So, I thought about it for a few days and finally decided it was time for me to leave New York and return to Kentucky.

Although my friends at the magazine thought I was nuts — and I sometimes thought that myself — it wasn't as hard a decision as it might have seemed. I was a dad now — my daughter Amy was born on Jan. 16, 1972, in Port Jefferson, Long Island — and Alice and I both felt she should be raised around family. Besides that, George Gill, the managing editor of the *C-J*, had offered me a job outside of sports that, hopefully, would allow me to see how I liked writing about other things.

I left on good terms. I certainly did not blame Andre for his decision. However, I admit it was a little tough watching Spitz become the story of the the Games. At least, he would have been the story had not Arab terrorists infiltrated the Olympic Village, taken several members of the Israeli team hostage, and killed them in a botched escape attempt. Because of that, Spitz, who was Jewish, came home after the last swimming event instead of staying for the closing ceremonies. Once back in the States, he gave me an exclusive interview that was picked up by the Associated Press.

I missed the 1976 Olympics in Montreal because I was out of sports, doing the *C-J's* general column, but I was sports editor when it was time for the 1980 Olympics and had received my credentials for the Games in Moscow. I was especially excited because of Mary T. Meagher, the teenaged swimming sensation from Louisville who had set world records in both butterfly strokes. Alas, however, President Jimmy Carter pulled out the U.S. team to protest the Soviet Union's invasion of Afghanistan. It may have been the right thing to do, politically, but it was a cruel blow for Mary T. and the other Olympians who had worked so hard for the right to go for the gold.

At the 1984 Summer Games in Los Angles, I realized how much I had been spoiled by my 1968 experience with *SI*. I spent three weeks in a small hotel room and was forced to rely on shuttles for transportation. But at least I finally got to see Mary T. win her golds, and I had an inside track with the men's basketball team due to my friendships with Head Coach Bob Knight and Team Manger C.M. Newton.

Knight hated the Soviets, and although they weren't there in repri-sal for our boycott of the 1980 Moscow Games, Knight coached every game as if he was preparing for World War III. That team was a wonder to behold. The starters were Sam Perkins of North Carolina and Way-mon Tisdale of Oklahoma at forward, Patrick Ewing of Georgetown at center, and Michael Jordan of North Carolina and Steve Alford of Knight's Indiana team at guard. The bench included Vern Fleming of Georgia, Alvin Robertson of Arkansas, and Jeff Turner of Vanderbilt.

After the championship game, Knight's players carried a coach off the floor, but it wasn't him. It was the legendary Henry Iba of Okla-homa State, whose 1972 Olympic team had been cheated out of the gold in Munich. And that leads to my best experience involving the Olympics.

The captain of the '72 Olympic team was Kenny Davis of George-town College in Kentucky, who got the spot that then was reserved for a player from AAU basketball. So, in 2010, when I was working as Scholar in Residence at Georgetown, I suggested to President Bill Crouch that the college should do something special for Kenny to hon-or the 40th anniversary of the travesty in Munich.

Dr. Crouch agreed and left it to me to come up with a plan. I took the idea to Kenny, and one thing led to another. We finally decided that since the 1972 team had never had an official reunion, we would invite the thirteen players, all of whom were still living, and assis-tant coach Johnny Bach (Iba and assistant Don Haskins had died) to come to Georgetown for an event that would include seminars, tours, and a banquet.

Once again, Dr. Crouch gave his approval but with the understand-ing that we would raise the money to pay for everything. We worked out a budget and figured we would need around $125,000 to cover the players' air travel, hotel accommodations, meals, and transportation. It was a daunting task — neither Kenny nor I were fund-raisers — but we were determined to give it our best shot.

It just so happened that Kenny was retiring from the Converse shoe company after forty years as one of its top sales representatives. He fig-ured he might be able to talk his boss, David Allen, into contributing $25,000 or so. Much to our shock and pleasure, Allen said Converse would contribute $100,000. Now those who were previously ambiva-lent about our idea suddenly began to pay attention.

We must have had God on our side because the weekend turned out even better than we had envisioned. We had a golf outing for the players, took them for tours and meals at Keeneland and Woodford Reserve, and put on a banquet at the Marriott Griffin Gate resort that was emotional and mesmerizing. Our speaker was Doug Collins, the former NBA coach and network TV analyst. In 1972, Doug was a skinny young guard from Illinois State who got knocked into a basket stanchion at the end of the gold-medal game against the Soviets. He rose groggily to his feet, went to the foul line, and knocked down two free throws to give the U.S. an apparent 50-49 victory.

Only three seconds remained when the Soviets inbounded the ball. Immediately Soviet players and coaches charged on the floor, apparently claiming they had not gotten a timeout they had requested between Collins' free throws. While the American players were celebrating, William Jones of Great Britain, the head of the Federation of International Basketball Associations (FIBA), came out of the stands, which he was not entitled to do under the rules, and took control of the chaos at the scorer's table.

Finally Jones told the referees to put three seconds back on the clock and let the Soviets inbound the ball again. This time a long shot bounced off the backboard and the U.S. players began celebrating again. But wait. Again exceeding his authority, Jones ruled that the clock had been reset incorrectly and ordered the Soviets be given a third chance with three seconds remaining. On the U.S. bench, Haskins told Iba that the U.S. team should just go to locker room and stay there. But Iba, fearing reprisals from the U.S. Olympic Committee, ordered the team back on the floor. This time they threw the ball the length of the floor to Alexander Belov, who laid it in to give the Soviets a 51-50 "victory."

As Collins talked, it was interesting to watch the players' faces. They had voted unanimously to not accept the silver medal because they had earned the gold, and they renewed that vow in Lexington. To this day, the silvers allegedly are stowed away in a vault in Switzerland. And now, all these years later, you could still see a flash of hurt or pain. Yet they also seemed to get a measure of redemption from the fact that somebody had finally decided to honor them.

When it was over, I was cleaning up some details when I noticed, out of the corner of my eye, that Kenny Davis was giving something to a few of the people who had helped us. He finally came up to me and said, with a smile, "You didn't think I'd forget you, did you?" And then he gave me the same ring the players had gotten, complete with my name printed on it. Finally, after months of work and planning, I lost it. I hugged him and cried.

Since that unforgettable night, Dwight Jones has died. He was the team's leading scorer, a 6-foot-10 load from Houston who ruled the paint. He brought his grandson to the reunion, and I'll always remember how eager that young man was to learn about what his grandpa had done all those years ago.

There was only one regrettable incident during the whole weekend, and I take the blame for it. At a press conference the afternoon of the banquet, I asked Tom Burleson, the 7-foot-4 center from N.C. State, to talk about the kidnapping and murder of the Israeli athletes. He told an incredible story about being in one of the tunnels under the Olympic Village when somebody put a machine gun to the back of his head and told him to turn and put his hands on the wall. He did so and then he heard the Israeli captives behind him as they were being led to the helicopters that would take them to the airport and their doom. He remembered their sobs of anguish.

At this point, Burleson had some sort of breakdown. He began crying and wailing. I was so stunned I didn't know what to do. But eventually he regained control, and we all hugged him and told him it was okay. It was disturbing to see how much he had been affected by the tragedy of forty years earlier. As Kenny Davis always says, "When you put it in perspective, all we lost was a medal; we didn't lose our lives."

Chapter Twenty-Three

THE GREATEST

The last time I saw Muhammad Ali, he was confined to a wheelchair and could barely speak. This was Oct. 1, 2015, when the top editors at *Sports Illustrated* came to Louisville to name a legends award in honor of the three-time heavyweight boxing champion and worldwide symbol of... well, let's just say that Ali was different things to different people.

For those of us who remembered Ali in the glory of his youth, it always was painful to see him in his decline. It was obvious that, slowly but steadily, he was losing to Parkinson's disease. First the mischievous light vanished from his eyes. Then his mighty voice became a whisper. Then he reached that state where he could barely acknowledge even those he recognized.

So, even though it was hardly a shock when he died on Friday, June 3, 2016, at age seventy-four, it still caused waves of sadness to resonate throughout the world, from the steel-and-glass canyons of New York City to the smallest villages in Africa to the war-torn and strife-ridden Middle East.

He was one of our own, born in Louisville on Jan. 17, 1942, as Cassius Marcellus Clay Jr., the son of a house painter, but he hadn't really belonged to us for a long time. He shocked the world not so much when he whipped Sonny Liston to win the heavyweight title on Feb. 25, 1964 — although that was a huge upset — but when he used his platform as heavyweight champion to reject his Baptist upbringing and join the Black Muslim nation led by Elijah Muhammad.

Unlike other Muslim sects, this group preached violence to the point that they murdered Malcolm X when he left the group and strayed from Elijah's teachings. That gave pause to the former Cassius Clay because he and Malcolm had become friends, but it didn't stop him from loudly and angrily challenging things in a society that had never before been challenged.

He was the epitome of "black is beautiful," a slogan of that time, and he was so charismatic that he become not only the most famous athlete in the world but also the most famous — or, infamous, as the case may be — spokesman against racism, injustice, and inequality wherever and however it existed.

When he refused to be inducted into the U.S. Army on April 28, 1967, on the grounds that he was a Muslim minister and a conscientious objector, many Americans, especially the veterans, regarded him as a coward and a draft-dodger. To this day, many have never forgiven him and refuse to acknowledge his vast accomplishments as a humanitarian.

Stripped of his championship by the world organizations that sanction boxing, Ali didn't fight from March 22, 1967, when he knocked out Zora Folley in Madison Square Garden, to Oct. 3, 1970, when he knocked out Jerry Quarry in the third round at Municipal Auditorium in Atlanta. His comeback was a gala social occasion for Atlanta's black community, which turned out in such finery that the fight had more the feeling of a movie premiere.

And so began the buildup to the fight everyone wanted to see — Ali against Joe Frazier, the bobbing-and-weaving slugger from Philadelphia who had taken over as heavyweight champion while Ali was in exile. It finally happened on March 8, 1971, in New York's Madison Garden, and it was such a huge event that *Life Magazine* hired Frank Sinatra to be one of its photographers. Ali wore red and white, with red tassels bobbing from his white shoes, and Frazier wore green and gold.

Knocked down for the first time in his pro career, Ali got up and fought to the end but lost on a 15th round decision. It was the first loss of his pro career, and it led Ali to re-invent himself as both a boxer and a person.

His chance to get his title back came on Oct. 30, 1974, in Kinshasa, Zaire. His opponent was George Foreman, a hard-punching younger man who had taken the title from Frazier. He appeared to be every bit as menacing as Liston had been more than a decade earlier. Yet Ali shocked the world again, knocking him out in the eighth round after allowing Foreman to punch himself into weariness in the early rounds. Ali called his strategy of taking punches the "Rope-a-Dope."

The win over Foreman showed that Ali was now relying more on his brains than his physical skills. He also had modified his behavior outside the ring. The Black Muslims were long gone from his life and so was the angry young man who did their bidding. The new Ali was kinder and gentler, a man who had come to believe in the power of peace and love.

After his upset of Foreman, he successfully defended his title ten times, including a 14th-round knockout of Frazier on Oct. 1, 1975. Known as the "Thrilla in Manila," that fight was such a slugfest that neither man was ever the same. Afterward, Ali said that it was as close to death as he had ever felt.

On Feb. 15, 1978, Ali faced Leon Spinks, a gap-toothed, converted light heavyweight, in Las Vegas. It was supposed to be an easy payday for the champ, and the jiggle around his middle showed that he hadn't bothered to get into top shape. Amazingly, Spinks won a 15th round decision that led some experts to proclaim that Ali was too old and needed to retire.

That night was special for me.

After filing my column for the next-day's *Courier-Journal*, I wandered over to Ali's hotel in search of a follow-up column. He had rented the entire top floor, and as soon as I stepped off the elevator, I was accosted by a couple of his bodyguards, who told me to turn around and get lost.

But then here came Ali's mother, Odessa Grady Clay.

"You leave him alone," she boomed at the musclemen. "That's Billy Reed from our hometown paper in Louisville. Ali is going to want to see him."

Five minutes later, I was seated next to Ali on his bed, scribbling notes as he told me how he was going to shock the world again by coming back to win the title a third time. Thanks to Mrs. Clay, as kind and gentle a soul as I've ever met, I got a "scoop" that was picked up by news outlets around the world.

That summer, Ali trained for his rematch with Spinks at his training camp in Deer Lake, Pennsylvania. Sensing that he had one more hurrah still in him, but that his career also was nearing its end, I went to Deer Lake to spend a few days.

Although I'm not sure Ali could ever call me by name, he knew my face and that I worked for his hometown newspaper. So, he let me get up in the dark of early morning and pray with him in his small mosque. He allowed me to go on runs with him, Ali in his heavy Army boots and me in my sneakers. He allowed me to watch him spar and interview him on a wide range of topics.

The only member of his entourage who wasn't there was trainer Angelo Dundee. That didn't bother me because I knew Angelo from other fights. But at Deer Lake, I got to know Gene Kilroy, Ali's long-time friend and go-fer; Luis Sarrera, his personal masseur; and Lana Shabaaz, his cook. It was fascinating to watch them work and to see how much they loved the champ.

When Ali arrived in New Orleans for the Spinks rematch, he was a different man from the one who had lost in Las Vegas. His condition was the best it had been in years. He was engaged, his agile mind focused on getting his belt back. As it turned out, it was Ali's last hurrah.

He carried Spinks for 15 rounds, seeming to revel in the noise and adulation emanating from the huge Superdome Crowd. At the end, he was the first man to claim the championship three times. It would have been the perfect time to walk away, as Mrs. Clay told me in a phone call after I had done a column urging him to retire.

A few days after the fight in New Orleans, Ali came home to be honored by the people who knew him best. Mayor Bill Stansbury asked me to be the emcee for a public ceremony in Cardinal Stadium at the Fairgrounds. I sat between Ali and Kentucky Governor Julian Carroll.

When it came time for Ali to speak, he was well into his remarks when a black man wearing a short-sleeved shirt appeared on the stage. I recognized his father, Cassius M. Clay Sr., and I thought he looked a bit tipsy. But Ali didn't miss a beat. Pointing at his dad, he said, "You want to see 'The Greatest'? It's not me; it's him right there."

He waited more than a year before defending his title against Larry Holmes, a former sparring partner, in Las Vegas. Although Ali looked healthy on the outside, it was an illusion, like the magic tricks he loved to perform. Unknown to anybody, he had been taking pills that deprived his body of water and energy.

Had he wanted, Holmes could have beaten Ali to a pulp. Instead, he let his idol retain his dignity as best he could. The fight went down in the books as an 11th-round knockout for Holmes, but it was over long before that.

When I ran into Holmes at the *Sports Illustrated* event honoring Ali, I thanked him for not embarrassing the champ that night. Replied Holmes, "There's more important things to me than money."

The final fight of Ali's career was a travesty held on Dec. 11, 1981, in the Queen Elizabeth II Sports Center in Nassau, the Bahamas. His opponent, the Canadian Trevor Berbick, was no better than a journeyman who wouldn't have lasted more than a couple of rounds against Ali in his prime.

The surroundings were unbelievably humbling for a man who had filled the great arenas of the world. The ring was a creaky old thing set up in the middle of a baseball field. A cow bell signaled the beginning and end of the rounds. There was no glitz or glamour, no women in long fur coats or men in velvet suits. But Dick Young of the *New York Daily News* and other prominent boxing writers were present, no doubt sensing the end, finally, for a man who would be remembered as far more than one of the fight game's all-time greats.

To the surprise of nobody, probably including Ali, Berbick won a 10-round decision. The next day, Ali refused to say that he was retiring. But he had to know it was over. He had to know that he would never again lace on a pair of Everlast gloves and light up an arena unlike any athlete ever.

The night he lit the torch to open the 1996 Olympic Games in Atlanta, I had my heart in my throat as he held out the torch in a shaking hand for all the world to see. It turned out to be his last significant appearance on a public stage.

After his retirement, I'd run into Ali every now and then when he came to Louisville. Sometimes he would show me a magic trick; other times he would tell a joke. But as time wore on and his disease grew more debilitating, he let his wife Lonnie become his spokesman and guardian.

I've often marveled over the fact that a black kid from Louisville, one who learned to fight only because his bicycle had been stolen, could become one of the most beloved — and hated — people in the world. I don't think the young Cassius Clay ever imagined being a symbol of hope and justice to people around the world. He just wanted to be The Champ, that's all.

But then he got swept up by a current of events and emotions that took him to places, physically and spiritually, that nobody could have envisioned when the young Cassius Clay was devoting his Saturdays to fighting on *Tomorrow's Champions*, the show on WAVE television, hosted by Uncle Ed Kallay, that was a showcase for the city's aspiring young fighters.

After his last fight, he used his role as the world's most famous Muslim to promote peace and love. He served several U.S. Presidents as an ambassador for one cause or another. He always had time for young people. As recently as the early months of 2016, he issued a statement deploring Republican presidential candidate Donald Trump's desire to ban Muslims from the U.S.

He will be remembered not only as a boxing champion but also as the champion of the poor, the underprivileged, and the disenfranchised around the world. Brash in his youth, he became humble as he aged. He prayed to Allah every day he was able. Thank heaven we have a museum in Louisville that will preserve his life, the controversial as well as the transcendent, for future generations.

Whether he knew my name or not doesn't matter. He recognized me, and I always will feel blessed that I sort of grew up with him, from the *Tomorrow's Champions* days through the Berbick fiasco. Most times I watched him from afar, but other times I sat on the edge of his bed or prayed with him in his mosque. He touched me unlike any other public figure ever has.

One night in the fall of 2015, less than a year before his death, I found myself standing behind his wheelchair in former U of L Athletics Director Tom Jurich's suite in Papa John's Cardinal Stadium. I was talking with Lonnie, and when she turned away to speak to somebody else, I just leaned over, kissed him on the little bald spot on the back of his head, and whispered in his ear, "God bless you, champ."

I don't know why I did that. But I'm glad I did.

Chapter Twenty-Four

BROADCAST NEWS
(AND ENTERTAINMENT)

The last few years of my checkered career, young people around Louisville have known me mainly as the old guy who was Drew Deener's co-host from 7 to 10 a.m. every Tuesday on ESPN680. This doesn't bother me a bit. To the contrary, I was grateful to Drew, a fellow Transylvania graduate, for giving me a forum long after I had reached retirement age. The third member of our team was Jim "Worldwide" Wombwell, our producer, call screener, soccer expert, and all-around good guy.

Because we grew up in different eras, Drew and I sometimes clashed about values. To him, I was often "Old School" in my thinking. To me, he was often too willing to dismiss things I thought were important. But we became very good friends who learned from each other and had a lot of fun in the process. I always will remember the Derby week morning on the backstretch of Churchill Downs when I did the "Julep Jump" with one of Lady Gaga's backup dancers. I am not making that up.

I've liked most of the radio and TV guys I've met over the years, both local and national. Heck, I covered Tom Hammond when he played ball at Lafayette High in the early 1960s. Of course, he went on to become a star at NBC sports, hosting everything from the Triple Crown to track-and-field at the Summer Olympic Games to Notre Dame football. He even did figure skating at the Winter Olympics.

Tom was a journalist instead of a show-biz star. He never let his celebrity go to his head and he always was prepared for his assignment. I put broadcasters such as Jim McKay of ABC and Dick Enberg of NBC in the same group. They always put the game or the story first, never letting their egos get in the way.

It was different, of course, with Howard Cosell.

I met Cosell when ABC had the rights to the Triple Crown races. He usually greeted me through a cloud of cigar smoke, and if I had a lady with me, he always would say something like, "Obviously, my dear, you know you can do much better." That was Howard being Howard. One year he was voted both the most-admired and most-hated announcer in sports. But he was smart, and as a former attorney, he was among the first to defend Muhammad Ali's refusal to be drafted into the Army on both legal and moral grounds.

One year when my friend Bobby Stallings was president of the Louisville Bar Association, he used his contacts at Churchill to get Howard to give a dinner speech to his group. He invited me to interview Howard one-on-one in his hotel room, which I did in the afternoon so I could get it in the next morning's paper.

Howard was testy at times, charming at others, but he filled up my notebook. The morning after his speech, he called Bobby from an airport somewhere and asked him to read what I had written about him. To me, that showed how insecure he was beneath all the bluster. Why else would the most famous personality in sports broadcasting care what I had said about him?

He must have liked it, though, because in his last book, Howard mentioned me on the list of writers he thought were good guys. He didn't list Red Smith, who needled him every chance he got. It was Red or one of the other New York guys who wrote, "Cosell is the only guy to ever change his name and wear a toupee so he could tell it like it is."

I think the best basketball-announcing team ever was NBC's triumvirate of Enberg, Billy Packer, and Al McGuire. They worked together from 1978 through 1983, when CBS outbid NBC for the rights to the NCAA tournament. Enberg was the catalyst who both called the game and played Packer, an Xs and 0s nerd, off McGuire, the native New Yorker who gave new definition to the term "color analyst."

I first encountered Al in 1968, when he brought his Marquette basketball team to Lexington to play Kentucky in the NCAA Mideast Regional semifinals in UK's Memorial Coliseum. He wanted to get under Coach Adolph Rupp's skin, and he succeeded beautifully, complaining about everything from his team's bench to its place on the scoreboard to the kind of ball being used. He even predicted that his 6-5 black center would get the first center jump over Kentucky's 6-8 white sophomore center Dan Issel.

Well, Issel got the tip and UK, goaded by Rupp and a raucous crowd, routed the Warriors, 107-89. That put them into the championship game against Ohio State the next night, and it turned out that the Wildcats had expended so much energy, both physical and psychic, on Marquette, that they let a less-talented Buckeye team steal their trip to the Final Four in Los Angeles on a last-second shot by Dave Sorenson.

Nine years later, in McGuire's last game as a college coach, Marquette gave him the NCAA title as a going-away present, beating North Carolina in the title game. The next year McGuire joined Enberg and Packer, and the first time he did a Kentucky game, he reinvented himself. The abrasive coach of 1968 was replaced by the smiling coach of 1978. He pulled it off, too, by praising Coach Joe B. Hall, Rupp's successor, and in 1979 dubbing freshman Dwight Anderson as "The Blur."

Knowing he needed to win over the press, Al called me out of the blue and said he wanted to take me to dinner. We went to a Mexican place in Louisville where Al blessed me with this piece of McGuire wisdom: "You know how you can tell if a Mexican place is good? Look at the waitress's ankles. If her ankles are dirty, it's a good restaurant."

We became very good friends. I once went shopping for toy soldiers with Al at a flea market in Freedom Hall, and he spent the night at my house a time or two. I also became his ghost writer, doing a magazine piece for him and working with him and Packer on a point-counterpart series of newspaper columns during an NCAA tournament.

Packer always was organized, insightful, and on time. With Al, it was a matter of him throwing out two or three random thoughts and then saying, "You do it in my style . . . you know what I want to say."

Once I got a package from him. When I opened it, a piece of old sheet music tumbled out. It was a song about Kentucky that he saw at a flea market, and it made Al think about me, so he bought it and mailed it. Nobody else has ever done anything like that for me. I didn't know the song from Adam, but it was the thought that counted.

I think most sports fans have a special place in their hearts for the play-by-play announcers of their favorite teams. That's because their voices are part of the background noise of our lives. They're always available to us no matter whether we're on the patio at home or driving the car. When I lived on Long Island, I sometimes went out on cold winter nights to find a place where I could pick up Cawood Ledford's U.K. basketball call on 50,000-watt WHAS in Louisville.

Back when TV was in its infancy, radio was the main connection between teams and their fans, and UK basketball was so popular that five or six stations or networks did live feeds from courtside. The ones I remember are Claude Sullivan of the Standard Oil Network, Cawood Ledford of WHAS840, J.B. Faulconer of the Ashland Oil Network, Jim Host of the Kentucky Central Network, Earl Boardman of WLAP in Lexington, and Jack Lorrie of WBLG.

By the mid-1960s, UK athletics director Bernie Shively had decided he wanted to start a UK Network with one lead announcer and a color analyst. But he didn't pull the trigger because he refused to choose between Claude and Cawood. By this time, Claude also had replaced Waite Hoyt as the Cincinnati Reds' lead announcer, and Cawood was doing freelance stuff for CBS and other companies.

Sadly, the choice was made for him when Claude died of a heart attack in December 1967, at age 42. So Cawood became the one and only "Voice of the Wildcats," a job he held through the end of the 1991–92 season. His final game was Duke's historic overtime win over UK for the championship of the Mideast Regional. Yes, that was the game where Duke's Christian Laettner caught a floor-length pass, pivoted, and put up a dagger that gave the Blue Devils the win as time expired.

The Reds, my favorite baseball team, always have employed good radio announcers. Back in the 1930s, Red Barber called the Reds games until he moved to Brooklyn to be the voice of the Dodgers. Hoyt was good on the play-by-play but superb during rain delays when he told stories about Babe Ruth, his teammate for years with the New York Yankees. After Claude died, the Reds went through a couple of play-by-play guys before settling on Al Michaels. And when Michaels left to become a network broadcaster, somebody in the front office was bright enough to hire Marty Brennaman, who at the time was doing basketball games for the Virginia Squires of the ABA.

Marty had the voice, the knowledge, the wit, and something novel: He described exactly what he saw on the field, the bad as well as the good. In other words, he was a reporter more than a "house guy" who never criticized the team that signed his checks. Marty belongs high on a list that, in my opinion, always will be topped by Vin Scully, who began working for the Brooklyn Dodgers in the early 1950s, moved to Los Angeles with them, and didn't retire until after the 2016 season.

Although I understand that young people are far more interested in careers in radio, TV, or social media than they are in the declining print media business, I still argue that good writing and reporting is the essence of good journalism. Some of the TV stars I admire the most — Hammond, McKay, Enberg, etc. — also were good writers. If you can write your own scripts, chances are you are going to be more effective than somebody who just reads another person's words.

Besides that, the ability to write well will be an asset if you decide to leave sports for another field. Lawyers often need good writers to help them with their briefs. Major corporations and government agencies all have good writers in their public-relations offices. And even radio and TV stations now need written content for their websites.

The day there is a radio or TV show devoted exclusively to women's sports, I'll believe that Title IX has achieved all its goals. But the truth is, women still get the short end of the stick in publicity and recognition. Radio and TV executives will tell you the size of crowds and ratings numbers just don't indicate there's much of an appetite for women's sports, except in a few markets where women's basketball has become about as popular as the men's game. Since radio and TV stations are governed by the bottom line, not Title IX, I don't see that changing much anytime soon.

In my opinion, the toughest job in sports broadcasting is calling horse races, especially the Kentucky Derby. Every year the race draws as many as twenty entries, and it's up to the announcer high atop the grandstand to memorize the names and the colors of the silks. Every announcer who has ever covered the Derby lives in fear of making a mistake, but that's what will be in the lead paragraph of his obit. The pressure finally got to the talented Tom Durkin, who retired from the business prematurely because of his nerves.

Unsurprisingly, some of the best race callers have come from Kentucky. Cawood Ledford and Claude Sullivan, besides doing UK football and basketball, were excellent race callers. So was Paul Rogers, who learned so much from Cawood at WHAS840 early in his career that he eventually became the voice of the Louisville Cardinals.

I also liked Mike Battaglia, who replaced Chic Anderson at Churchill when Chic left to join the New York Racing Association. It was Chic, the pride of Henderson, who called Secretariat's incomparable performance in the Belmont Stakes, telling the crowd and the national TV audience that "he's running like a tremendous machine!" Mike rarely made a mistake and probably knew the game better than anybody because he grew up with it. His dad, John, was the longtime general manager at Latonia (now Turfway) Park and the long-gone Miles Park in Louisville.

For many years, Keeneland didn't have a public-address system on the rather stuffy but quaint theory that its fans should be knowledgeable enough to identify the horses by the colors of the jockey silks. For years, Mike called the Keeneland races solely for the guys who posted the numbers of the leaders on the electronic tote boards. When the demand for an announcer became too loud to ignore, Keeneland hired Kurt Becker, who had a NASCAR background, and he surprised everyone with how well he could call real horse power instead of the mechanical sort.

I've enjoyed my work with Drew Deener on ESPN680 and my *Conversations with Champions* series on KET. But newspaper ink runs through my veins. Even if I'd had the skill for a fulltime career in broadcasting, I would still have picked writing. And that's why they call me "Old School."

Chapter Twenty-Five

THE COLLEGE SPORTS SWAMP

When the news broke in late 2017 that the FBI had filed criminal charges against four assistant college basketball coaches for colluding with the Adidas shoe company to funnel illegal payments to recruits, Notre Dame coach Mike Brey said, "I don't know if we can get any lower than the situation that we're in now. We've had this underworld as a part of the fabric (of college basketball) for a long, long time."

He was absolutely right.

Except that big-time men's basketball and football programs will find a way to go lower unless the college presidents, through the NCAA, mandate the most comprehensive reform movement in sports history.

Of course, we all know the reason for the widespread corruption. It's right there in the Bible, I Timothy 6:10: "For the love of money is the root of all evil."

Universities and colleges, which are supposed to be bastions of enlightenment and honor, have sacrificed their academic integrity at the altar of athletics dollars. Who would have ever imagined that North Carolina, one of the nation's great public universities, could have ever allowed students, including many athletes, to get credit for passing a class that didn't exist — and then spend $18 million defending the fraud against NCAA sanctions?

I don't know exactly when it all began to change. Was it 1972, when the federal government's Title IX mandate forced public-school athletics departments to support women's sports at the exact same level as men's sports? This was a landmark decision that changed the sports culture. But because there was no female sport equivalent to football, the biggest sport of all, it forced athletics directors to scramble for new money to make the numbers work.

At the University of Kentucky, a bright young entrepreneur named Jim Host bought the university's radio rights and parlayed that into a sports marketing empire that eventually included the NCAA and many of its most notable members — Notre Dame, Texas, Tennessee, etc. Host showed his clients how to use their powerful brand names to line up corporate sponsors that were willing to spend big money to be associated with football and men's basketball, particularly the NCAA men's tournament and the Final Four.

While Host was giving conference commissioners and athletics directors the blueprint for increasing their bottom lines, the Entertainment Programming & Sports Network (ESPN) went on the air in 1979. I first became aware of it that fall when former network announcer Jim Simpson called the Alabama-LSU football game for ESPN. Looking at the network's literature in the press room, I figured ESPN was some crazy cable TV venture — who could imagine a channel devoted to sports and games 24/7? — and would quickly fade from view. But I grossly underestimated how many Americans were addicted to sports or gambling or some combination of both.

As ESPN was shaking up the culture of sports television, building a large inventory of college sports, a shoe and apparel company based in Beaverton, Oregon, was challenging the monopoly that Converse and its Chuck Taylor All-Stars had enjoyed in the basketball shoe market since World War II. Known for its trademark swoosh, Nike pulled a major coup by signing Michael Jordan to a huge endorsement contract after he left North Carolina in 1984. As he became the best basketball player in the world, Nike put out a line of shoes known as "Air Jordans." Since every kid wanted to "Be Like Mike," to cite one of Nike's promotional slogans, Nike blew Converse out of the basketball waters by the late 1980s.

In order to get an early toehold with the college and NBA stars of the future, Nike and its rivals, Adidas and Under Armour, began holding lavish summer camps and all-star games for the best players and supporting the AAU teams for which they played in the summer. An unintended byproduct of the camps and all-star games was that they provided forums for the agents and flesh peddlers to get their hooks into the players and their families, some of whom were "on the take" for illegal payments.

While the shoe companies were gaining power and influence that the NCAA and college presidents largely ignored, the NBA, which had never been forced to establish a viable minor-league system, passed a rule that prohibited players from going straight from high school into the NBA draft, as stars such as Lebron James and Kobe Bryant had done. This created the so-called "one-and-done" culture in which super-talented players who had no interest in getting a college degree nevertheless got scholarships from schools willing to exploit their talents for a year or until they turned nineteen and became eligible for the NBA.

Nobody took advantage of this loophole more effectively than John Calipari at Kentucky, who took so many "one-and-done" players that he virtually had a new roster every season. Pure and simple, Kentucky became the NBA's No. 1 farm team, and even though Calipari's large paychecks were signed by UK, which wanted him to win national titles, he candidly admitted his main goal was getting his recruits into the NBA.

Unfortunately, Duke Coach Mike Krzyzewski gave up fighting the "one-and-done" mindset and joined it. This is the same Coach K., of course, who wouldn't allow Christian Laettner's jersey to be retired and hung in the rafters of Cameron Indoor Stadium until he had earned his degree.

And then there were all the sordid stories about players abusing drugs and alcohol, which often led to abuse of wives and girlfriends. As much as their programs tried to rationalize their aberrant behavior, sometimes they had to dismiss them. But there always was another place willing to give them a second chance because they were good players.

The money from TV, the shoe companies, and other sources has jacked up coaches' salaries to obscene levels. If a pro team wants to pay a coach that kind of money, you can chalk it up to America's unhealthy addiction to sports. But there's something different about a college coach making that sort of money when professors are grossly underpaid and many students are going deep in debt to finance their educations.

Inevitably, the culture of corruption in college football and men's basketball became so pervasive that the public, and even the media, came to cynically believe that everybody cheats to some degree, so why get bent out of shape about it? I never accepted that argument, but with every passing year, I also have a harder time refuting it.

So, here's the crucial question: Is it possible to win and compete in today's big-time college sports world without making ethical and moral compromises?

As Mike Brey indicated, this is the bomb that has been ticking inside college football and men's basketball for years. Sadly for college sports, the NCAA, i.e. the college presidents, ignored it until, finally, the FBI got involved.

In the fall of 2017, the FBI's office in the Southern District of New York filed criminal charges and arrested assistant basketball coaches at four major programs (Auburn, Arizona, Southern Cal, and Oklahoma State). They were accused of funneling money from shoe-and-apparel giant Adidas to the families of prized recruits.

Suddenly it was a whole new ball game. It's one thing to deal with investigators from the bloated, inept bureaucracy known as the NCAA but quite another to run afoul of the FBI. A fifth Adidas client, Louisville, also was implicated, leading to the firing of basketball coach Rick Pitino and athletics director Tom Jurich. This was one of the most difficult things I've ever had to confront. I considered Tom and Rick to be friends at least partly because I could never see them getting involved in scandals. But that began to change with the news that Rick was being extorted by a woman whom he apparently had impregnated. Jurich stood by him again when a "madame" revealed that U of L assistant Andre McGee had paid her to have sex parties in the dorm named for Pitino's late friend, Billy Minardi. The FBI scandal left U of L no choice. The FBI promised that more criminal charges and arrests were to come, striking fear in the hearts of the programs that have cast their lot with Nike, by far the biggest supplier of shoes and clothing to college athletics departments.

At this point, I must tip my hat to Dale Brown, the outspoken former LSU basketball coach who has been talking for years about the NCAA and its failure to control corruption.

Of all the coaches I've ever known, Dale was one of the most difficult to figure out. I'm still not sure I've done it. Because of the impoverished circumstances of his youth in North Dakota, Dale inevitably became a champion of poor kids who also were great basketball talents. He pointed out, correctly, the hypocrisy and lack of compassion in many NCAA rules.

Once the money genie is out of the bottle, it's all but impossible to put it back in. So, those who love big-time college basketball and football must find solutions — and they are there, if only the college presidents would find their moral compass and do the right things.

If I were given the power to change college sports, I would first re-fuse to sanction the summer camps and all-star games sponsored by the shoe companies.

I would deal with the one-and-done travesty by going back to the rule by which freshmen are ineligible for varsity competition.

I would stipulate that no coach or athletics director could be paid a salary higher than the best-paid academic dean.

I would insist that all money for shoe-and-apparel companies go into a fund for athletes who suffer debilitating injuries while playing in college.

I would streamline and simplify the rules book. I would speed up due process for programs accused of rules violations.

I would encourage conferences to declare that any program found guilty of rules violations could not be on TV for a year.

These moves would go a long way toward restoring the balance be-tween athletics and academics. They would remind us that universities are in the education business, not the sports business.

As a journalist, I noted one aspect of the Louisville mess that pretty much summed up the problem. At the time the FBI scandal hit, the student newspaper, *The Cardinal*, was begging for $25,000 to stay in business.

That sort of money is pocket change at a university that could pay its basketball coach $5 million or so per year. It's unacceptable, especially when it's considered that there's a far greater likelihood that the student newspaper will produce graduates who will contribute more to society than the varsity basketball players.

Understand, we need entertainers in our society. But we don't need them as much as we need doctors, lawyers, teachers, scientists, and, yes, journalists.

Chapter Twenty-Six

FINAL THOUGHTS

As I was wrapping up this book, I went to see *The Post*, the movie about the *Washington Post's* decision to print the so-called *Pentagon Papers* in 1971. The movie stars Meryl Streep, who is wonderful as *Post* publisher Kay Graham, and Tom Hanks, almost as good as executive editor Ben Bradlee. Graham had to decide between Bradlee's impassioned pleas to print the classified government documents detailing decades' worth of lies about the Vietnam War and the advice of her business people to not publish because of retribution from the Nixon administration and its deep-pocket supporters.

The movie delighted me on a nostalgic level because of its newsroom scenes. Editors smoked, rotary phones rang incessantly, manual typewriters clattered, and teletype machines spat out wire copy on long rolls of paper. Beyond that, it was nice to see newspaper people depicted as courageous heroes instead of "enemies of the state," to borrow a quote from the Trump administration. All over again, the movie made me proud that circumstances had thrust me into this profession that is mandated by our Constitution and has protected the public welfare since the founding of our nation. Mrs. Graham sided with Bradlee, of course, and her decision was vindicated by the U.S. Supreme Court.

Of all the nation's publications, the *Post* and the *New York Times* have done the best jobs of carrying their core principles into the internet age. They have not compromised their journalistic integrity, and the sensational reporting by both about the various scandals that have rocked our nation the last couple of years has encouraged all of us who worry about the future of journalism. We may be well on the way to a day when print newspapers are extinct. But now we know that great journalism can be practiced on the Internet. It's just harder to find, that's all, because of all the bogus bloggers and website operators posing as legitimate journalists.

And by the way, I can't think of *The Post* without remembering a story told by David Vance. When he was general manager of the Kentucky Colonels of the ABA, the team had a player named Wendell Ladner, who was much stronger in the looks department — he once posed semi-nude for a poster — than the brains department. So, once, as the Colonels were preparing to land in Washington, D.C., Ladner looked down and saw this tall monument.

"What's that?" he asked Vance.

"Wendell," said Vance, gazing down at the Washington Monument, "that's the *Washington Post*."

"Oh, yeah." Ladner nodded. "I've heard about that."

I've mentioned a lot of my friends in this book because I decided a long time ago that, in lieu of money, I wanted to leave them a memory. I want all of them to be able to tell a story that begins with "I remember the time that Reed and I. . . . " Of all these friends, however, none has shared more experiences with me than Bill Malone, who loves sports more than anybody I've ever known, myself included.

I met Bill in 1963 or '64 through Cal Bates, one of my Kappa Alpha Order fraternity brothers at Transylvania. He came up to me one day and said, "I know a guy you've got to meet; he knows more about sports than you do." So, Bill and I met between games at one of the high school triple-headers that used to be held in UK's Memorial Coliseum, and both of us immediately saw a kindred spirit in the other.

Although he was struck by polio as a kid growing up in Allen, near Pikeville, Bill didn't let that keep him from living as normal a life as possible. He recovered to the point that he could play golf or go boating. He became everybody's best friend, or so it seemed, because he was so decent and polite. And smart. Lord, is he smart. He was the valedictorian of his senior class at Centre, and I'm convinced that if he had been as devoted to, say, finding a cure for a disease as he's always been to beating the point spread, he could have done it.

As it was, he became a CPA and one of the founding members of Deming, Malone, Livesay, & Ostroff, now one of the state's leading accounting firms. It was a natural choice for him because accounting, like sports, is all about numbers. Plus, he was able to be his own boss and earn enough money to make trips to exotic locations, such as Saratoga,

San Diego, Las Vegas, Monte Carlo, Detroit, and Miami. For fun, Bill put together syndicates to buy Thoroughbreds that would be trained by his friend Vickie Foley.

As smart as he is, Bill couldn't make himself adapt to computers, which probably hastened his retirement from the accounting business. I didn't much like them, either, but I didn't have any choice if I wanted to remain sports editor of The C-J. So in the late 1970s, I reluctantly retired my trusty Olivetti portable typewriter and more or less learned to use this big, ugly, metal box known as a Teleram.

I'm certain that lugging that thing through airports stretched my arms by an inch or so. They also were grossly unreliable. I remember a time at Muhammad Ali's training camp in Deer Lake, when I spent hours laboring over a column I thought was pretty good. But just when I was ready to finish the last paragraph, a sudden electrical storm caused the lights in my motel room to blink. When I looked at the computer screen, my story was gone.

I can't begin to tell you the discipline it required to sit down, gather myself, and start again. I remembered the note Tom Callahan, then of the *Washington Star*, left me after his computer failed, and I let him borrow mine. "I now know," he wrote, "that I am incapable of either murder or suicide."

The big lie about computers, and the way the bosses convinced the ink-stained wretches to accept them, was that they would enable us to push back deadlines because they were so fast. At some papers, perhaps that was true. But at the *Courier-Journal*, computers had the opposite effect, especially after Gannett bought the paper and began using the building at Sixth and Broadway as a central layout and printing station for several of its papers.

The deadlines were moved up, not back. Today most things that start after 7 p.m. will not be in the next day's paper. It's not because it can't be done because we did it for decades with far more primitive tools. It's just that Gannett is committed to a business model that places no importance on getting the news to local print subscribers as soon as possible.

But this, too, could change. When I review what I've seen happen in the business over the last twenty-five years, I realize there's no way to predict what will happen in the next twenty-five. All I know for sure is that the Internet isn't going away. Neither are smart phones, social media, and Dick Tracy wristwatches (if you don't know who he is, you'll just have to Google it). The challenge for the journalists of today and tomorrow is to effectively use all the new media without compromising the ageless principles of quality journalism.

I freely admit it's much more challenging to be a sports journalist today. Besides having to deal with tweets and podcasts and all the technological stuff, sports journalists have to know something about the law, crime, drugs, abusive behavior, business, and economics. In other words, the sports world is a microcosm of our larger society, and people attempting to cover sports cannot exist in a vacuum or some fantasy world.

Since the 1920s, kids have looked to the sports and entertainment worlds for heroes and role models. It used to be easy because there seemed to be so many of them. One reason for that could be that the media of those days didn't report on the personal lives of celebrities. But I also believe that, in those simpler days, sports and entertainment stars weren't as spoiled as they are now

Having said that, I love the games and athletes as much as ever. When you've been around as long as I have, people always want to ask you about the best this or that that you ever covered. So here I will offer a few random lists of the best I've covered. If I never saw a player compete in person – my friend Ralph Beard was before my time, for example – I cannot include him or her on these lists.

Five best sports bars or restaurants (some now gone) – The Green Jacket, Augusta, Ga.; The Wishing Well, Saratoga Springs, N.Y.; The Derby, Santa Anita, Cal.; Pat's Steak House, Louisville, Ky.; Esposito's Tavern, Long Island, NY.

Best five college basketball players – Lew Alcindor and Bill Walton, UCLA: Christian Laettner, Duke; Oscar Robertson, Cincinnati; Pete Maravich, LSU. (Michael Jordan did not become Michael Jordan until he became a pro).

Best five college basketball coaches – Adolph Rupp, Kentucky; John Wooden, UCLA; Dean Smith, North Carolina; Mike Krzyzewski, Duke; Bob Knight, Indiana.

All-time baseball team – Johnny Bench, Reds, catcher; Stan Musial, Cardinals, first base; Joe Morgan, Reds, second base; Ozzie Smith, Cardinals, shortstop; Brooks Robinson, Orioles; third base; Hank Aaron, Braves, left field; Willie Mays, Giants, center field; Roberto Clemente, Pirates, right field; Ted Williams, Red Sox, DH.

Best five baseball announcers – Vin Scully, Dodgers; Marty Brennaman, Reds; Mel Allen, Yankees; Jack Buck, Cardinals; Harry Caray, Cardinals and Cubs.

All-UK basketball team – Dan Issel, Jamal Mashburn, Cotton Nash, Anthony Davis, Kenny Walker.

All-U of L basketball team – Wes Unseld, Butch Beard, Darrell Griffith, Charlie Tyra, Gorgi Dieng.

Boys' All-State Tournament team – King Kelly Coleman, Wayland; Wes Unseld, Louisville Seneca; Darrell Griffith, Louisville Male; Richie Farmer, Clay County; Larry Conley, Ashland.

Five best sports writers – Red Smith, New York Times; Jim Murray, Los Angeles Times; Dan Jenkins and Frank Deford, Sports Illustrated; Dave Kindred, Louisville C-J, Washington Post, Atlanta Journal-Constitution.

Five Best Sports Movies – Hoosiers, The Natural, Bull Durham, Field of Dreams, Semi-Tough.

Five best college football coaches – Paul "Bear" Bryant, UK, Texas A&M, Alabama; Nick Saban, LSU and Alabama; Steve Spurrier, Florida and South Carolina; Ara Parseghian, Notre Dame; Woody Hayes, Ohio State.

Five best college sports information directors – Roger Valdiserri, Notre Dame; David Housel, Auburn; Kenny Klein, Louisville; Don "The Fox" Bryant, Nebraska; Haywood Harris, Tennessee.

Five best college basketball arenas – Cameron Indoor Stadium, Durham, N.C.; Memorial Coliseum, Lexington, Ky.; Freedom Hall, Louisville, Ky.; Madison Square Garden, New York City; Crisler Arena, Ann Arbor, Mich.

Five best Heisman Trophy winners – Harschel Walker, Georgia; Roger Staubach, Navy; Archie Griffin, Ohio State; Barry Sanders, Oklahoma State; O.J. Simpson, Southern Cal.

Five best players who did not win Heisman – Peyton Manning, Tennessee; Joe Montana, Notre Dame; Tom Brady, Michigan; Lou Michaels, Kentucky; Jim Brown, Syracuse.

As I've glided into the twilight years, I jumped all over that mulligan that life gives dads, if you're lucky. In other words, I've tried to make up for all the things I missed when my daughters Amy and Susan were growing up by getting as involved as I can with my grandchildren.

My daughter Susan's sons, Shephard and Sam, are still too young to have accomplished much except be so cute they break your heart. But my daughter Amy's older daughter, Caroline, is a performing artist who even got to appear with the Moscow Ballet in the winter of 2017-'18. And her younger daughter, Lucy, amazes me with her poise and skill as a gymnast. Both have accomplished far, far more than I had at their ages.

Amy's husband, Rob Frederick, has become my friend as well as my son-in-law. He's the executive in charge of sustainability at Brown-Forman, a position he uses effectively to promote responsible drinking and environmental protection. My girls' mother, my first wife Alice, re-married a wonderful man named Crawford Wells. He could not have been a better stepfather to my girls, and I will always be grateful.

I've never tried to push sports or journalism on anyone in my family. Amy probably came the closest to taking up my line of work. In her undergraduate days at Duke, she worked for the student newspaper, *The Chronicle*, and loved it. But her calling was art history, so she dumped the newspaper business in favor of getting a master's and a doctorate in that field from Case Western Reserve in Cleveland. The day she got her doctorate, the entire family was there and it was one of the proudest days of my life. She used that doctorate to become a full-time professor at Centre College.

Susan turned out to have more of a knack for business, so after graduating with a degree in that field from UK, she embarked on a career that has taken her around the country. She has lived and worked in Colorado, California, Massachusetts, Maryland, and, of course, Kentucky. At every step of the way, she learned something that helped her move upward and onward. For the past several years, she's worked for Sanofi Genzyme, a pharmaceutical company based in Boston, and they have rewarded her good work in many ways, being especially supportive when she decided to adopt the boys.

So I sit here and watch with wonderment. I haven't done anything to deserve all this. I'm still writing about sports, the same thing I was doing in high school. But I don't go too far down that road because there are just some things in life that I'm not capable of understanding, such as why hot dogs do, indeed, always taste better at the ballpark.

Earlier I mentioned friends. These days one of the high points of any week is having Monday lunch at Selena's Restaurant with old pals such as Malone, John Brewer, Ronnie Galloway, Skip Connell, Hal Smith, Dan Renkes, Nick Burrice, Bud Hughes, Wade Wearren, Bill Glaser, and Max Mascarich. Oh, the lies we tell.

Finally, I would simply like to say "thank you" to everybody who has even taken a few moments from their lives to read something I've written. When you stop and think about it, it's rather presumptuous to think you have something to say that will be of interest to hundreds of thousands of people almost every day, week after week. But I tried it, just the same. and feel so humbled whenever I run into somebody who remembers something I wrote that made them laugh or cry, get mad or glad or just think.

I would like to say that I wouldn't trade my experiences for all the gold in Fort Knox, but I'm not going to end this by lying. I'm one of the few civilians who actually have been inside the vault – the government opened it to the media in 1974 to prove the gold was still there – and, trust me, the sight of stacks and stacks of gold bars will widen your eyes a bit. But, heck, if I had all that gold I would never have gotten to hang out at all kinds of joints, from posh ones like Elaine's to the dives around race tracks, with newspaper guys, the best company in the world.

It's not gold, but it's been a pretty rich way to go through life.

WILLIAM F. "BILLY" REED

National Award-Winning Newspaper and Magazine Journalist,
Radio Talk Show Host, Public Speaker, Investigative Reporter,
Communications Specialist and Author of 18 books

Education Career

Adjunct professor, Bellarmine University (2016-Present)

Adjunct Professor, University of Louisville Sports Administration Program (2013-'14)

Executive Scholar in Residence, Georgetown College (2009 – 2012)

Adjunct professor, National Center for Sports Journalism, Indiana University (Fall, 2009-2010)

Special Assistant to the Provost (Kentucky State University (2008-'09)

State Government

Special Assistant to the Attorney General (2007)

Executive Director of Communciations, Kentucky Commerce Cabinet (2004-'05)

> (*Oversaw the public-relations functions of 16 state agencies, including Parks, Tourism, Fair Board, Fish & Wildlife, Center for the Arts, and Sports Authority.*)

Director of Communications, Kentucky Horse Racing Authority (2004)

Print Journalism

Sports Illustrated

> Senior Writer, 1988-1998
>
> Special Correspondent and Staff Writer, 1968-1987

Louisville Courier-Journal
   Sports Editor, 1977-1986
   General Columnist, Special Projects Writer, 1972-1977
   Staff Writer, 1966-68
Lexington Herald-Leader
   Sports Columnist, 1987-2001
   Assistant Sports Editor and Staff Writer, 1959-1966
The Sports Media Team
   Executive editor, 2010-Present

Freelance Writing

SI. Com, ESPN College Basketball Encyclopedia, People Magazine, Time, The Washington Post, The Miami Herald, The San Diego Times-Union, TV Guide, The Sporting News, Inside Sports, The Baltimore Sun, The Blood-Horse, Thoroughbred Times, Business First, San Francisco Chronicle, The Louisville Sports Report, Kentucky Monthly, Basketball Times

Radio & TV Experience

Radio Talk Show Host at ESPN680, WGTK, WHAS, WTMT, and
   WAVE in Louisville, Kentucky.
Senior commentator at WAVE3 Television.
Recurring TV commentaries for WHAS TV in Louisville and WKYT
   TV in Lexington.
Numerous appearances on ESPN, CBS, ABC, The History Channel
   and CNN.

Books (author or contributor)

Hurstbourne Country Club: The 50th Anniversary (Butler Books, 2016)
The KFC Yum! Center (Butler Books, 2011)
Celebrating 54 Years of Freedom Hall (Butler Books, 2010)
The Monarchs and The Great American Rock n' Roll Dream (Butler
   Books, 2009)
Lombardi as I Knew Him (Triumph Books, 2006)
Golden Boy: The Paul Hornung Story (Simon & Schuster, 2004)
Billy Reed: My Favorite Derby Stories (Butler Books, 2003)
Famous Kentuckians (Courier-Journal Books, 1977)
Born to Coach: The Denny Crum Story (Courier-Journal Books, 1986)

Hello Everybody, This is Cawood Ledford (Host Communications, 1992)

Newton's Laws (Host Communications, 2001)

History of University of Louisville Football (University of Louisville Press, 1999)

The Final Four (Host Communications, 1988 and republished in 2003)

Thoroughbred: A Celebration of the Breed (Simon & Schuster, 1988)

The Best of Sports Illustrated 1972 (Little, Brown, 1973)

A Century of Kentucky Derby Coverage (Courier-Journal Books, 1974)

Best American Sports Stories (1978 and '79)

Transition Game: The Integration of Basketball in Kentucky (Host Communications, 2002).

Keeneland: First 50 years (Harmony House, 1986)

Honors and Awards

Kentucky Journalism Hall of Fame

Kentucky Athletic Hall of Fame

U.S. Basketball Writers Hall of Fame

Transylvania University Hall of Fame

Henry Clay High School Hall of Fame

National Headliners Club for Investigative Reporting

National Headliners Club for Consistently Outstanding Sports Columns

Sigma Delta Chi National Award for General Reporting

Eight (8) time recipient of Kentucky Sports Writer of the Year

Two (2) Best of Louisville@ awards for newspaper columnist

Transylvania University Distinguished Alumnus

Transylvania University Distinguished Service Award

Tom Hammond Media Award

Thoroughbred Industry Awards

Three (3) Eclipse Awards for outstanding thoroughbred racing coverage

Eight (8) Red Smith Awards for Kentucky Derby Coverage

Old Hilltop Award

Charles Englehard Award

Walter Haight Award for Career Excellence

Two (2) Bill Leggett Awards for Best Breeders' Cup Magazine Story
Two (2) David Woods Awards for Best Preakness Story
Dean Eagle Award for Derby coverage
Florida Breeders Award

Organizations

Vice-Chariman, Kentucky Basketball Hall of Fame
Former Board Member, Kentucky and Southern Indiana Leukemia &
    Lymphoma Society
Past President, Kentucky Thoroughbred Media
Past President, National Turf Writers Association
Past Selection Committee Chairman, Kentucky Athletic Hall of Fame
Kentucky Representative on Heisman Trophy Selection Committee
National Turf Writers, U.S. Basketball Writers, Football Writers of
    America
Past board of directors member for Muhammad Ali Center,
    Kentucky-West Virginia Cystic Fibrosis Foundation, and
    Transylvania Alumni Association
Parish Council St. Frances of Rome

Personal

Born in Mt. Sterling, Kentucky, July 12, 1943
Graduated Transylvania University, BA English, 1966
Served in U.S. Army Reserves, 1966-1971
Hobbies include golf, reading, poliitics
Father of daughters Amy (Duke '94) and Susan (Kentucky '96)

INDEX